THE ACTS OF GOD

The Good
The Bad &
The Ugly

Prince Aremi Amachree

AuthorHouse™
1663 Liberty Drive, Suite 200
Bloomington, IN 47403
www.authorhouse.com
Phone: 1-800-839-8640

© *2009 Prince Aremi Amachree. All rights reserved.*

No part of this book may be reproduced, stored in a retrieval system, or transmitted by any means without the written permission of the author.

First published by AuthorHouse 5/12/2009

ISBN: 978-1-4343-9543-6 (sc)
ISBN: 978-1-4343-9544-3 (hc)

Printed in the United States of America
Bloomington, Indiana

This book is printed on acid-free paper.

All scripture quotations, unless otherwise indicated, are taken from the King James Version®.

Scripture quotations marked (NIV) are taken from the HOLY BIBLE, NEW INTERNATIONAL VERSION®. NIV®. Copyright© 1973, 1978, 1984 by International Bible Society. Used by permission of Zondervan. All rights reserved.

Prince Aremi Amachree
P.O. Box 426
Bogota, NJ 07603 U.S.A

Cover design by: Prince Aremi Amachree

Contents

Acknowledgment ix
Introduction xi

Chapter One
He Created Everything 1
   Fundamentals: 1
   Heavens, Earth, Good, and Evil 2
   People of Various Kinds 2
   The Dumb, the Deaf, and the Blind 4
   Seasons 5
Questions to Ponder 8

Chapter Two
He Causes all Things 9
   Fundamentals: 9
   Covering for the Body—The Naked Test 10
   Languages of Many Kinds—The Confusion 10
   He Instituted Death 12
   The Birthright—The Esau and Jacob story 14
   The Journey of the Exodus 15
   The Good, the Bad, and the Ugly 18
   God of Everything 22
   Deliverance 23
   Desire 30
Questions to Ponder 34

Chapter Three
He Causes all Things—The Joseph Story 35
   Fundamentals: 35
   God's Perfect Plan for Joseph 36
   The Dialogue between God and Joseph 37
   Joseph Promoted from Slave to Ruler 40
   The Great Famine from God 42
   Chaos in Transit 45
   God Sent 46
   The God of Multiplicity 47
Questions to Ponder 50

Chapter Four
He Curses..51
   Fundamentals: 51
   The Truth About Curse 52
   Real Curses from God..53
Questions to Ponder...56

Chapter Five
He Wounds..57
   Fundamentals: 57
   Affliction of the Innocent 58
   The Barren Woman 60
   God's Afflictions 61
   Evil Spirit from God...66
   Hate or Choice 67
Questions to Ponder...69

Chapter Six
He Kills..70
   Fundamentals: 70
   Noah's Ark – The Second Beginning 71
   Killing in Diverse Measures..72
   Killing in the Wild—God's Style 73
   Instrument of Death—Warfare 76
   Women and Children Too...80
   Weapons of Destruction..81
   God with His Own Hands 85
Questions to Ponder...87

Chapter Seven
He Deserves the Credit and the Blame 88
   Fundamentals: 88
   Blame Me 89
   Fulfilling Your Destiny 91
   Consequence of Disobedience...94
   Give God the Credit 97
   Some prophesies to come:..101
Questions to Ponder...102

Chapter Eight
He Tempts..103

Fundamentals: 103
Who Wants to Know? 104
Questions to Ponder 106
Chapter Nine
He is Merciful 107
Fundamentals: 107
The Harvest 108
Only God 109
Your Only Sacrifice 110
Questions to Ponder 112
Conclusion 113
Fulfilling God's Plan for Your Life 116

Acknowledgment

Glory to the Almighty and Invisible God, the One and Only Immortal God, the Everlasting God, the One who created everything according to His good pleasure, for the revelation and understanding He has given me, to Him, be glory, honor and power forever. Amen.

And

To my beautiful wife, Princess Olga Amachree, who took the time to do the at-home, firsthand editing of the book before it was sent to the outer world for a second look. Thank you honey for your love and support, I love you dearly!

Introduction

For too long, many have preached and taught the word of God with a great deal of inconsistency. As a result, mankind is drifting away from the knowledge of God. Therefore, I found it reasonable to write about some of the things that are separating us from the knowledge of God; in the hope that we may have a better knowledge of our Creator.

Some of our so-called ministers and religious leaders have drifted so far away from the word of God that in many events today, they have no explanation whatsoever. This is because, what they would say, would contradict what they had said in the past—this leads them to stay mute instead of contradicting themselves and their understanding and integrity been questioned. In other cases, they intentionally mislead the people to maintain their own integrity so as to defraud the people. Please note that we are all developing in the knowledge of God—no one knows it all.

This book is intended to bring you close to the understanding of the Kingdom of Heaven and to give you a balanced understanding about the kingdom of Heaven. The book intends to justify God in ALL that He has done and to expose the weaknesses of the human understanding about the kingdom of Heaven. Take a journey with me to a place called Truth and Revelation. At the end of this journey, you will have a better understanding about the Kingdom of God, and you will have better answers to questions such as:

- Why did God create the heaven and the earth, especially the earth?
- Why did He create man and beast?

- Did God have certain expectation when He created man and beast?
- Did God predefine the purpose of His creations before He created them? If so, does God change His mind when you refuse to do what is expected?
- Why did God create both good and evil? Is evil also good, and it's just that we have not understood it?
- Does God actually know the future at all times?
- Does anything happen that God did not plan?
- Can you refuse evil God has asked you to do?
- Does anything happen without God?
- Does God create each person for a specific purpose?
- Can anything stop God's plan?
- Why do people die?
- Did God originally plan for man to live forever in the flesh?
- Has the human brain fully grown to the point God wanted it?

These and many more complex questions will be answered by the time you have finished reading this book. The book outlines whether or not God is the God of everything or whether He's the God of just some things and not others. That is, whether God is the good, the bad, and the ugly.

Please do not ask me who am I to talk to God like this. I am not talking to God; I am talking to you! Some of these questions, if not all, have been asked before even in the Bible. In the days of the Apostle Paul, human understanding was too low for Paul to answer the question "Why does God blame us?" The human brain and understanding are more developed than in the days of Paul. Yet even at this time, not everything can be revealed to us. However, the answers to some of these questions can be revealed now.

You have known the first steps to reach the kingdom of Heaven (the goodness); for you to know the steps after these steps, you need to read this book. It will help you understand those steps. Take a journey with me to this Truth.

Before we go deep into complex matters, though, I want to make sure you understand that God is the creator of the universe and everything therein. The whole universe came into fullness from one creation after another and one creation into another. Sometimes the death of one creation is the birth of another creation.

"In the beginning God created the heaven and the earth." Gen. 1:1.

"Before I formed you in the womb I knew you..." Jer. 1:5 NIV.

"The LORD killeth, and maketh alive: he bringeth down to the grave, and bringeth up. The LORD maketh poor, and maketh rich: he bringeth low, and lifteth up. He raiseth up the poor out of the dust, and lifteth up the beggar from the dunghill, to set them among princes, and to make them inherit the throne of glory: for the pillars of the earth are the LORD's, and he hath set the world upon them." 1 Sam. 2:6–8.

"I have loved you, saith the LORD. Yet ye say, Wherein hast thou loved us? Was not Esau Jacob's brother? saith the LORD: yet I loved Jacob, And I hated Esau, and laid his mountains and his heritage waste for the dragons of the wilderness." Mal. 1:2–3.

As you read along you will notice that less emphasis is made to those books referred to as poetry in the Bible. Although they contain some highly regarded proverbs and parables and some valid writings, reasoning, history, and opinion, this book is not focused on the opinions of poetry. It is rather focused on the irrefutable, mighty power and authority of God.

In chapter one, we will talk about the creations God has made. Chapter two talks about whether God causes all things or just some things. In chapter three, we will have a closer look on whether God causes all things by using the life of Joseph as a paradigm. Chapter four will look into whether God curses or not. In chapter five, we will have an opportunity to discuss whether God can wound or afflict you. Chapter six will set the stage to discuss the issue of whether God kills. Chapter seven will give us the revelation of who takes credits and who takes blames in everything that happens. In chapter eight, we will talk about one of the most controversial but least talked about topic of whether God tempts or tests His creations. And finally, in chapter nine, we will have the privilege to look into the mercy of God and what is in the mercy of God for us as humans.

My prayer for you is that after reading this book, you will have a better understanding about the Kingdom of Heaven, and that you will know and have a better relationship with God, far greater than you ever had before. Knowing God is this: that you come to know the purpose for which He has created you for, and that you accomplished it! This is what I call knowing God.

Chapter One

He Created Everything

Fundamentals:

"In the beginning God created the heaven and the earth." Gen. 1:1.

"And the LORD God formed man of the dust of the ground, and breathed into his nostrils the breath of life; and man became a living soul. And the LORD God planted a garden eastward in Eden; and there he put the man whom he had formed. And out of the ground made the LORD God to grow every tree that is pleasant to the sight, and good for food; the tree of life also in the midst of the garden, and the tree of knowledge of good and evil." Gen. 2:7–9.

"And out of the ground the LORD God formed every beast of the field, and every fowl of the air;…" Gen. 2:19.

"And the LORD God caused a deep sleep to fall upon Adam, and he slept: and he took one of his ribs, and closed up the flesh instead thereof; And the rib, which the LORD God had taken from man, made he a woman, and brought her unto the man." Gen. 2:21–22.

"Before I formed thee in the belly I knew thee; and before thou camest forth out of the womb I sanctified thee, and I ordained thee a prophet unto the nations." Jer. 1:5.

Some have believed and others have yet to believe that God created everything. Since many of the creations and formations would be discussed in this book, it would make no sense without discussing the creation and their starting places first. In this chapter, we are going to identify some of the creations, their sources and how they were established.

Heavens, Earth, Good, and Evil

Have you ever asked yourself why God created the Heavens and the Earth—especially the Earth, since the Heaven is His Fortress? I want you to go into the mind of God for a moment. Did God have certain expectations when He created all creations? The Bible says that God created them in and for His pleasure. God seems to be a craftsman or artist—someone who likes to create something out of nothing and see how it'll look. Did God had a WOW moment—when He found out that what He has created was looking better than what He was expecting? I am sure there were certain expectations.

Why did God make both good and evil in the first place? Is evil another name for opposite? Does opposite necessarily mean bad or evil? You and I know that is not true. Then, why should we call evil bad? Have you ever wondered why the Bible says rejoice always? Well, depending on the language you use or the circumstance you're in, evil does not always equate to bad even with the limited means of communication we have as humans today. For example, it was after evil came upon the inhabitants of the Promised Land that Israel took ownership of the land. For Israel, this was good, whereas the previous inhabitants saw it as evil. A simple, modern-day example is the relationship between a car driver and the tow truck businessman. While the car driver hopes that his car doesn't break down, the tow truck businessman is hoping that the car breaks down so that he may have a business. All to the glory of God and the hope they all have in Him!

People of Various Kinds

There are different kinds of people and different kinds of purpose. Each person is created and assigned a specific purpose. With racial and ethnic tensions around the world, one would think it was an error in God's part to have created people of various kinds in the creation. It is, however, not about the class or names people are calling you; it is rather about what you have been created to fulfill. Some names are tolerable in some societies and in other societies they are not. Do you remember some of the names you have in your society? For example there are names such as doctor, nurse, black, white, Hispanic, Chinese, firefighter, pilot, homeless, shoplifter, criminal, prostitute, alcoholic and drug addict, police, farmer, and president. Each person's purpose and fulfillment is what God is concerned about. The name or title people call you may be degrading and sometimes unbearable. They may, however, not see that the name is giving you the protection you need to fulfill your purpose—that purpose for which God has created you. Sometimes the name you are being called is a mirror image of your purpose, though the name is superficial—because those calling you that name has no knowledge of your purpose or inner being.

Consider this woman named Rahab. Her story may sound to you like a science fiction novel or a CIA covert operation; however, it is not. Rahab was a harlot in Jericho when Joshua sent in spies to spy the land for a takeover. *"... And they went, and came into an harlot's house, named Rahab, and lodged there."* Jos. 2:1. Though she may have been known as a harlot, the name or title given to her gave her a strategic dwelling place in Jericho, and she did exactly what she was purposed to do at that time. And that was to welcome the spies, protect and care for them without being caught by the king and his army, who sought them and demanded that she brings them out. *"And the woman took the two men, and hid them, and said thus, There came men unto me, but I wist not whence they were."* Jos. 2:4.

James referred to her actions as righteousness (faithful to what you are supposed to do). Her righteousness was not that she was a harlot but because she fulfilled her purpose and cared for the men. *"Then she let them down by a cord through the window: for her house was upon the town wall, and she dwelt upon the wall. And she said unto them, Get you to the mountain, lest the pursuers meet you; and hide yourselves there three days, until the pursuers be returned:*

and afterward may ye go your way." Jos. 2:15–16. This woman was not only a harlot, she was a betrayer. She had just betrayed her own country. In today's world or even at that time, if she were to be caught hiding the spies, that might result in a very long prison term up to life, if not a death sentence. But no, she was credited righteous for fulfilling her purpose, lodging the spies—not the name she was being referred by her fellow citizens. She was on the victory side of God's plan. And what was God's plan in this case? It was to destroy the inhabitants of Jericho so that the Israelites could take over Jericho and dwell therein.

Opinion poll: Was Rahab a bad or a good person? Was she assigned to be in this position by God before the spies came to the city? Was her assignment ordained by God, or she was just doing them a favor? I mean, was she working for God? Was her harlotry an exception? Be careful, you judges! I'm sure you know my answer already.

Why then, did God create both good and bad people? As good complements evil, so also one person complements another whether different or alike. A good person complements a bad person and a bad person complements a good person. Good purpose complements evil purpose, and evil purpose complements good purpose. One purpose complements another. Despite that something is unfavorable to you doesn't make it a bad thing. Think about it!

The Dumb, the Deaf, and the Blind

"It is an attack from the enemy!" Does this phrase sound familiar to you? Everything we perceive as negative or unfavorable, we consider it to be from the enemy. Let me reveal the power of God to you, so that you'll stop calling God an enemy. God revealed to Moses regarding the mouth, the ears, and the eyes in a response to Moses' complaint he was not a good speaker: *"…Who hath made man's mouth? or who maketh the dumb, or deaf, or the seeing, or the blind? have not I the LORD?"* Ex. 4:11. And if I may add, it is the same God who teaches each one of us to say what we say. So, why are we going about talking as though the dumb, the deaf, and the blind are not a work of God?

The Acts of God

"And I will harden Pharaoh's heart, and multiply my signs and my wonders in the land of Egypt."

The fact that we don't know the WHY does not negate the purpose of God's creation. Even the hardness of a man's heart is from God. God said to Moses, *"And I will harden Pharaoh's heart, and multiply my signs and my wonders in the land of Egypt."* Ex. 7:3

Here is a 'why'—to multiply His signs and wonders in the land of Egypt. God continued to harden Pharaoh's heart so that the Egyptians followed the Israelites into the opened Red Sea and were consumed. Let me expose your understanding a little bit: The hardness of Pharaoh's heart—was that strength or a weakness of Pharaoh? So next time, before you criticize someone for being soft or hard, remind yourself that God has a purpose for that person's softness or hardness. Pharaoh's hardness of heart contributed to our belief and revealed to us today the magnitude of the power of God. On the contrary, Pharaoh's softness and refusal to go after the Israelites would have added to our unbelief today. In retrospect, did Pharaoh really have control of his mind if God could harden it as He wanted?

So regardless of your condition, make no mistake, count it all joy, because God has created you and He has a plan and purpose for you.

Seasons

"To every thing there is a season, and a time to every purpose under the heaven: A time to be born, and a time to die; a time to plant, and a time to pluck up that which is planted; A time to kill, and a time to heal; a time to break down, and a time to build up; A time to weep, and a time to laugh; a time to mourn, and a time to dance; A time to cast away stones, and a time to gather stones together; a time to embrace, and a time to refrain from embracing; A time to get, and a time to lose; a time to keep, and a time to cast away; A time to rend, and a time to sew; a time to keep silence, and a time to speak; A time to love, and a time to hate; a time of war, and a time of peace." Ecc. 3:1–8.

There is nothing under the heaven which God has not created or purposed—nothing happened by accident or by luck. God has created everything for its season and its appointed time. Let's examine the case of a barren woman, does every woman have to bear a child? Should a woman who has yet to have a child be considered passed her time? No. It simply means her God-appointed time has not come. Furthermore, some are created not for child-bearing but for other purposes too many to be mentioned here. Nevertheless, if a woman bears no child, she should thank God for that and seek to have the understanding and wisdom of God as to why she bears no child. It is only God who can shut off a woman's womb or determine the time when she should have a child. We are going to take this discussion in a different standpoint when we talk about afflictions using two women (Rachel and Hannah) who were considered barren. While they were considered barren by human beings, they gave birth at the appointed time of God.

This appointment of time expands around every area of life. God created everything and appointed time for their materialization. This included kings and leaders—both the evil and the good minded. Nebuchadnezzar was viewed and described to be terrible and evil minded because he exiled and kept the Israelites captive for seventy years. Though he was and is still being viewed as evil by those who were afflicted through him and those who lack the ways of God, he was a God appointed leader and a servant of God. *"I have made the earth, the man and the beast that are upon the ground, by my great power and by my outstretched arm, and have given it unto whom it seemed meet unto me. And now have I given all these lands into the hand of Nebuchadnezzar the king of Babylon, my servant; and the beasts of the field have I given him also to serve him. And all nations shall serve him, and his son, and his son's son, until the very time of his land come: and then many nations and great kings shall serve themselves of him. And it shall come to pass, that the nation and kingdom which will not serve the same Nebuchadnezzar the king of Babylon, and that will not put their neck under the yoke of the king of Babylon, that nation will I punish, saith the LORD, with the sword, and with the famine, and with the pestilence, until I have consumed them*

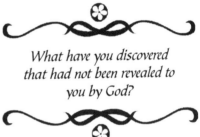

What have you discovered that had not been revealed to you by God?

by his hand." Jer. 27:5–8. He came to being at the appointed time and fulfilled his God-given purpose.

The foundation of a house is laid only once. The same is true for all God's creations. God laid the foundation of everything in six days and He created man to manage them. Many believe that God is still creating. I say to those people, look closely—God has finished creating. What follows that creation today is reproduction, discovery or revelation and understanding of what had been created. I don't even like that word 'discovery' that much—What have you discovered that had not been revealed to you by God?

For example, God explicitly created elements X and Y, but did not create element Z in that order but rather implicitly; however, God had made it possible that when elements X and Y are combined, they formed element Z. This becomes a new revelation or reproduction—it is not a new creation. In this example, X and Y may be a male and a female. While Z is a child or children. Someone once asked me, if God has finished creating, what would I call a new born? My answer was simple and precise: a reproduction. A reproduction of what has already been created: man and woman. Despite the fact that scientist had just got the knowledge of a planet out there, doesn't mean God has just created it. It simply means scientist have just got the revelation that this planet exists. Until you gain the understanding of something, you would never know it exists.

The foundation of everything that has been and is to be have all been laid by God and are set for their appointed time. Some of which had been discredited and later found to be credible because the understanding of that creation became evident. For this reason, we can conclude that God created everything—whether we see them as good, bad, or ugly.

Questions to Ponder

Is there anything God has created that should be called evil?

Is there anything God has created that should be called bad?

What is God's purpose in creating different kinds of people?

Did God create bad people?

Chapter Two

He Causes all Things

Fundamentals:

"The LORD killeth, and maketh alive: he bringeth down to the grave, and bringeth up. The LORD maketh poor, and maketh rich: he bringeth low, and lifteth up. He raiseth up the poor out of the dust, and lifteth up the beggar from the dunghill, to set them among princes, and to make them inherit the throne of glory: for the pillars of the earth are the LORD's, and he hath set the world upon them." 1 Sam. 2:6–8.

"…I will have mercy on whom I will have mercy, and I will have compassion on whom I will have compassion." Ex. 33:19 NIV.

"See now that I, even I, am he, and there is no god with me: I kill, and I make alive; I wound, and I heal: neither is there any that can deliver out of my hand." Deu. 32:39.

"And the eyes of them both were opened, and they knew that they were naked; and they sewed fig leaves together, and made themselves aprons. And they heard the voice of the LORD God walking in the garden in the cool of the day: and Adam and his wife hid themselves from the presence of the LORD God amongst the trees of the garden." Gen. 3:7–8.

We have talked about the creations; let's now turn our attention to how events of all kinds are formed. In this chapter, we are going to use several events in the Bible to demonstrate it is the power of God that causes all things to occur. It is about time we end the ignorance of sharing this authority between God and Satan.

Covering for the Body—The Naked Test

What is wrong with being naked? Do you think God planned a world without clothing? It is possible. Was the event in Genesis 3 the way God introduced the importance of clothing to mankind? Or are we saying that, right from the beginning, things got out of God's hand? Did God think He had created a monster after man misbehaved?

Was not the invention of clothing a stage in God's making? I want you to keep this in mind: the human understanding is still being developed as of today. God can ONLY talk or communicate with you at the level that you can understand. Even in terms of media, the medium in which God communicates with us has changed. Today God speak to us through radio, television, internet, telephone, and many other media. In the days of Adam, Abraham, Moses, and many in the beginning, God was more PHYSICALLY present. Now, what other way would have been possible for God to communicate with Adam and Eve about the importance of clothing? What you should bear in mind is that Adam and Eve were like newborn babes with no knowledge of anything. They now had passed their first test—that is, how to make clothes for themselves.

For generations past, our focus has been on disobedience of Adam and Eve. Instead of focusing on the achievements Adam and Eve made in their early years of existence—that is, making clothing for the body. This event of Adam and Eve making cloths was a step in the creation not a misstep. Otherwise, we should conclude that God did not know what Adam and Even were to become.

Languages of Many Kinds—The Confusion

Today, nations and advocates of various kinds are effortlessly trying to make the whole world become one government, market, economy, border, religion, and even one language—it is called globalization. Did you know, in those days when everyone in this world was speaking one language, God found it to be not a good idea? Let's examine what happen in Genesis chapter eleven, starting from verse one—*"And the whole earth was of one language, and of one speech. And it came to pass, as they journeyed from the east, that they found a plain in the land of Shinar; and they dwelt there. And they said one to another, Go to, let us make brick, and burn them thoroughly. And they had brick for stone, and slime had they for morter. And they said, Go to, let us build us a city and a tower, whose top may reach unto heaven; and let us make us a name, lest we be scattered abroad upon the face of the whole earth. And the LORD came down to see the city and the tower, which the children of men builded. And the LORD said, Behold, the people is one, and they have all one language; and this they begin to do: and now nothing will be restrained from them, which they have imagined to do. Go to, let us go down, and there confound their language, that they may not understand one another's speech. So the LORD scattered them abroad from thence upon the face of all the earth: and they left off to build the city."* Gen. 11:1–8.

In one language and in one accord, the people decided to build tower so that they could reach heaven (building a skyline). They did the same thing we do today with such things as lighthouses so that when we go afar, we can have a guiding post to return if we have to. I don't think God at this time wanted people to go and return. God instead wanted people to fill the whole earth, therefore He expected them in those days to scatter on the face of the earth. Mankind instead wanted to stay in his comfort zone.

It is easy to see an example of this in the life of Abraham, whom God sent to a land Abraham knew not. As Abraham arrived in Canaan, there came famine that drove Abraham into Egypt. God continued to stretch Abraham beyond his limit (as we think of it) in order to show him the splendor of the world. Through this process, Abraham knew not only the land God had prepared for him to dwell in, but he also knew the surroundings of the land he now lived in.

Does God know something that we don't know about the benefits of a multi-language world? Yes. A typical example of this is the behavior of corporations in our societies today; corporations today seek diversity in their organizations because they have come to the realization that when different viewpoints and opinions are brought together, the best solutions are found for their problems. God established this principle in order that mankind would bring different viewpoints to cultivate this planet. Those who do not have the understanding of this simple principle would think it was a bad move for God to cause the world to have multiple languages. The language you speak plays a significant role on how you would translate a subject matter. Thus, it enables you to have a different view than another person on the same subject matter. This is not to say that people who speak the same language do not also have differences of opinion. Furthermore, different languages create different agendas.

God created languages of various kinds when society was speaking just one language. If you think that multi-languages in this world are a bad idea, then you may be saying that God established what was wrong. I am convinced that multi-languages are for the good.

He Instituted Death

"And the LORD God said, Behold, the man is become as one of us, to know good and evil: and now, lest he put forth his hand, and take also of the tree of life, and eat, and live for ever: Therefore the LORD God sent him forth from the garden of Eden, to till the ground from whence he was taken. **So he drove out the man***; and he placed at the east of the garden of Eden Cherubims, and a flaming sword which turned every way, to keep the way of the tree of life."* Gen. 3:22–24.

Though He made us in His own likeness, yet He did not want us to live forever. Why did God change His mind and send Jesus so that we may have everlasting (not in the flesh) life? After all, He prevented man from eating on the tree of life. If the tree of life is knowledge, God has prevented man from having that knowledge. If it is a plant, seed, or anything else, God has prevented man from getting a hold of it. Did the act of man change God's plan for man's life? Did God plan for man to live forever without death in the flesh? The answer is No!

"And the LORD said, My spirit shall not always strive with man, for that he also is flesh: yet his days shall be an hundred and twenty years." Gen. 6:3.

This is another scripture that shows where God said man must not live forever or His (God) Spirit shall not be in man's flesh forever. God, knowing the weakness of the flesh, declared that at certain point in man's life, there is no reason to remain in a flesh that would no longer have strength. In this same message, God also revealed that there has to be a population control in the earth. God therefore declared that

The Acts of God

Imagine for a second that no one had died since the beginning of time.

man should live for a hundred and twenty years. Imagine for a second that no one had died since the beginning of time.

What would have been the population of the earth? Today there are over six billion people on the face of the earth; you'd also need to add in the total deaths since the beginning of time (How many are they?). This is already enough to clear the remaining forests for housing. This would undoubtedly lead to starvation since people, from lack of understanding, would build houses instead of using the land for farming. We are already living in a generation that does not know the importance of man and that uses man's food to create fuel for cars, thereby starving man! Death therefore is part of the overall plan of God. Jesus has shown us that death is part of the equation.

However, there are some people that will not see the grave at the end of their sojourn. *"And Enoch walked with God: and he was not; for God took him."* Gen. 5:24. In today's world, the disappearance of Enoch would have raised a state, national, or even worldwide Amber Alert (an electronic message alert usually sent to various locations in the United States when someone has been abducted or gone missing). A message would have gone out in an Amber Alert system with sentences like this: *"Enoch has been declared missing. He was last seen with God. God may be armed and dangerous. Anyone who sees him or them should call 1-800…"* That means that if God were found, He would be questioned regarding Enoch—and possibly arrested. Those who understand the things of God will know that walking with God is a good thing. For God to spare you, not to see death is not only a good thing, but a great and wonderful thing. And to others, it is terrible to just disappear and not have a grave named after them.

Is it better to die and be buried or to be taken by God without seeing death itself? I can tell you that most people would prefer it if, when they die, we see them being lifted up and taken to heaven rather than that they are simply buried or taken by God without anyone noticing. People like to make a show of everything. What I am painting for you to see is this: it is God who makes some die and have a grave named after them; it is the same God who makes some disappear and have no grave named after them. It was God Himself who declared that man should not live forever in the flesh—in the flesh! The spirit of man will live forever, either in heaven or in hell.

In the past, many have lived their lives filled with fear of death. Jesus came and rescued them from that fear—He demonstrated that death is part of the equation of life and that everyone should be happy to partake of it as they journey to fulfill their destiny.

The Birthright—The Esau and Jacob story

"And the children struggled together within her; and she said, If it be so, why am I thus? And she went to enquire of the LORD. And the LORD said unto her, Two nations are in thy womb, and two manner of people shall be separated from thy bowels; and the one people shall be stronger than the other people; and the elder shall serve the younger." Gen. 25:22–23. God had just revealed to Rebekah the wife of Isaac what He had planned for the twins in her womb (Esau and Jacob). Keep this in mind as we dissect this story.

When it was time for her to give birth to the children, Esau was first delivered. *"And after that came his brother out, and his hand took hold on Esau's heel; and his name was called Jacob: and Isaac was threescore years old when she bare them."* Gen. 25:26. Why was Jacob holding Esau's heel? Was it because he wanted to come out first? Did he know something about the weak human reasoning in terms of birthright and the plan of God even before he was born?

Let's look into the drama of how God dealt with the weak thinking of man in terms of blessing and seniority. This needed to be dealt with; otherwise Jacob would not be treated right as God wanted him to be treated by people and even his father Isaac. First, Isaac with his open eyes would not give blessing to Jacob as he would to Esau; therefore, Isaac had to be blinded to give Jacob the blessing God wanted Isaac to give Jacob. Next, to avoid confusion between Esau and Jacob, Esau had to give up his birthright willingly. Now we're ready to bring the plan of God to fruition. *"And Jacob sod pottage: and Esau came from the field, and he was faint: And Esau said to Jacob, Feed me, I pray thee, with that same red pottage; for I am faint: therefore was his name called Edom. And Jacob said, Sell me this day thy birthright. And Esau said, Behold, I am at the point to die: and what profit shall this birthright do to me? And Jacob said, Swear to me this day; and he sware unto him: and he sold his birthright unto Jacob. Then Jacob gave Esau bread and pottage of lentiles; and he did eat and drink, and rose up, and went his way: thus Esau despised his birthright."* Gen. 25:29–34.

This is a typical example of how God deals with us based on our understanding. For man, it is the first that comes out between twins or among multiples who is considered oldest. For God, that is not the case. God chose whom He wants to use. By the way, who told man that the first to come out is the oldest? Could it be that the first to be conceived is the oldest, and they don't always come out in that order?

When it was time for Isaac to give the birthright blessing, Jacob presented himself as Esau and took the blessing of the birthright because Isaac at the moment was blind. Though Isaac was a mere man, God had deposited in him a blessing that must be discharged to someone. For Isaac, it was for Esau his first son, and for God, it was for the one He had chosen—Jacob. Granted, man does not live by bread alone! Did Esau say the right thing when he said to Jacob that he was at the point of death and what profit would his birthright do for him if he were dead? Some of you have crucified and condemned Esau for his decision. What was the value of his birthright if he were dead? Some have said Jacob took the blessing that belonged to his brother Esau. Is that what God said when He said the older shall serve the younger? Do all these drama add or remove anything to what God had revealed to Rebekah their mother? Did Rebekah tell Isaac, her husband, about God's plan, and Isaac knew and was rebellious against God's plan? Was Isaac blinded for this purpose by God? Was Jacob a deceiver or was he in accordance with God's plan? I tell you, the plans of God cannot be understood by our mere thinking.

Do you think God really cares about who has the birthright and who doesn't? So that you know, God does not care about birthright; otherwise He would not have chosen Isaac (among Abraham's sons), David, Solomon, and many others—even Joseph—as we'll see in the next chapter.

The Journey of the Exodus

Pay careful attention to this passage, because it'll change your understanding forever. It is contrary to what you have heard in the past. After several years in Egypt, it was time for Israel to depart and return to the Promised Land. *"And it came to pass, when Pharaoh had let the people go, that God led them not through the way of the land of the Philistines,* **although that was near***; for God said, Lest peradventure the people repent when they see war, and they return to Egypt: But God led the people about, through the way of the wilderness of the Red sea: and the children of Israel went up harnessed out of the land of Egypt."* Ex. 13:17–18.

So it was God who chose the long path for the exodus; it was God who thought that the people would need exposure to war. Although God moved them away from danger because the Philistines were nuts, He also make sure that they received the training they needed and that they were not exposed to war too soon in the journey. God took them through a path where He could give them the training or exposure they needed to survive the land they were heading to possess.

When God made the decision of the longer route, Israel had not started rebelling against Moses or the commandments of God. Therefore, it was not Israel's rebellion that led to their extended stay in the wild as we had been made to recognize. In fact, it was more than rebellion, as you'll see later.

Was God right when He made this decision to extend the journey? In Exodus 14, when the Israelites saw that the Egyptians were advancing nearer to them, the Israelites cried and said to Moses, is it that there were no graves in Egypt that you brought us out here to die in the wilderness? They had said to him while in Egypt to leave them alone, that they would serve the Egyptians instead of going on the exodus. They said they would rather be slaves in Egypt than go back to Canaan. In fact, in the book of Numbers chapter 14, due to hardship in the wilderness, the Israelites decided to appoint a captain to lead them back to Egypt because they didn't know what was up with Moses and Aaron, who were their leading men who brought them out of Egypt. Of course they fought wars during the long journey; however, they did not encounter wars too soon and they did not run away from the wars that they faced afterwards because they had been prepared for fighting their own wars in the process of the long journey. Though in the process of the long journey many lives were lost, the relationship with God was made stronger and the ultimate goal was achieved. And that goal was to be of good courage, have better relationship with God, not return to Egypt, and conquering the Promised Land Canaan.

If God had revealed to the Israelites from the beginning that some of them would die in the wilderness, would they have joined the exodus?

As we have seen, the plan for the long route started in the early stages of the exodus. Do you still think it was because of Israel's rebellion and unbelief? Are you saying God did not know the Israelites would misbehave? God planned this route even before the Israelites began to disobey Moses and the commandments of God. When it was time for God to remove good apples from bad apples sometime in the journey, God said to Moses *"Because all those men which have* **seen my glory**, *and* **my miracles**, *which I did in Egypt and in the wilderness, and have tempted me now these ten times, and have not hearkened to my voice; Surely they shall not see the land which I sware unto their fathers, neither shall any of them that provoked me see it…* **Tomorrow turn you, and get you into the wilderness by the way of the Red sea…Your carcases shall fall in this wilderness; and all that were numbered of you, according to your whole number, from twenty years old and upward which have murmured against me… And your children shall wander in the wilderness forty years, and bear your whoredoms, until your carcases be wasted in the wilderness.** *After the number of the days in which ye searched the land, even forty days, each day for a year, shall ye bear your iniquities, even forty years, and ye shall know my breach of promise. I the LORD have said, I will surely do it unto all this evil congregation, that are gathered together against me: in this wilderness they shall be consumed, and there they shall die…"* Num. 14:22–35.

If God had revealed to the Israelites from the beginning that some of them would die in the wilderness, would they have joined the exodus? If God told the elders that they would not reach the land of promise, would they have left Egypt? When God told Abraham that his descendants would possess the land He has promised, God did not say it would be all the people that would exodus Egypt. God said Abraham's descendants; as the fathers that perished in the wilderness were descendants of Abraham, so also were their children. Was God planning for those fathers to reach the Promised Land? Absolutely not! Those people's lives and behavior had been influenced by their Egyptian masters. Now you have seen the reasons for the lengthy journey. God was not planning on sending corrupted minds and lazy people into a land He cared for. But in all these events, God chose the Israelites to set as an example for us. If God had told them this is what He planned to do, would they have agreed and gone along with the plan? None of them would have left Egypt. God will only speak to you based on your understanding level. Was it God's plan right from the beginning to eradicate those unbelievers and the corrupt during the journey? You bet! By the time of the second census in the journey of the exodus (Numbers 26), those adults had all perished in the wilderness.

It was not that Israel was so stupid that they wandered in the wilderness for forty years. Moses said to Israel regarding their limited understanding about the exodus: *"Yet the Lord hath not given you an heart to perceive, and eyes to see, and ears to hear, unto this day"* Deu. 29:4. Israel wandered in the wilderness because that's what God has planned; He kept them in the dark for forty years. *"And the LORD's anger was kindled against Israel, and he made them wander in the wilderness forty years, until all the generation, that had done evil in the sight of the LORD, was consumed."* Num. 32:13. Though it was portrayed as though Israel's disobedience was why God made them wander, it was the appropriate way in which God could communicate with them at that time. God knew from the beginning those He wanted in the land. In the later years of mankind, God is communicating with man differently because our understanding has developed to a higher level. Keep in mind man is still in the making—the understanding of man is still being developed.

In truth the journey of the exodus accomplished these key elements: revealed God to Israel, strengthened and encouraged the Israelites, eradicated the corrupt, and finally prepared them to take the Promised Land. The journey, the years spent, the timing, those to die in the journey are all planned by God to fulfill His eternal purpose.

The Good, the Bad, and the Ugly

One of the greatest phenomenon God demonstrated to the Israelites and to us during the journey of the exodus was His authority to separate the sea to let the Israelites cross over toward the Promised Land—a power that even brilliant scientists could not figure out how God made it possible. But one thing God told the Israelites about the Promised Land during the several years with much good, suffering, pain, and afflictions in the wilderness was to eradicate the current inhabitants in the land. When Israel arrived at the Promised Land, Israel did not drive out all the inhabitants of the land that they possessed. God told them to drive the people out of the land, but they did not obey God's instruction. What will Israel do to reverse their land battle with their neighbors today? Nothing, and it might even get worse than what they see today. Because God has said it: *"But if ye will not drive out the inhabitants of the land from before you; then it shall come to pass, that those which ye let remain of them shall be pricks in your eyes, and thorns in your sides, and shall vex you in the land wherein ye dwell.* **Moreover it shall come to pass, that I shall do unto you, as I thought to do unto them.***"* Num. 33:55–56. Although it was God who said *"I will not drive them out from before thee in one year; lest the land become desolate, and the beast of the field multiply against thee. By little and little I will drive them out from before thee, until thou be increased, and inherit the land."* Ex. 23:29–30. Now it is on the shoulders of Israel that they didn't drive all of them out. The hint of God's plan is in His message to Israel, *"Moreover it shall come to pass, that I shall do unto you, as I thought to do unto them."* No one has a permanent residence in this planet. People come and go. And God is not expecting any one of us to come here and claim territory and permanent residency. So Israel's suffering today is a process people have faced before, either forcefully or willingly as they live on this planet.

God said to the Israelites that He is doing all of these not because of Israel's righteousness but because of the wickedness of the people dwelling in the land. *"Understand therefore this day, that the LORD thy God is he which goeth over before thee; as a consuming fire he shall destroy them, and he shall bring them down before thy face: so shalt thou drive them out, and destroy them quickly, as the LORD hath said unto thee. Speak not thou in thine heart, after that the LORD thy God hath cast them out from before thee, saying, For my righteousness the LORD hath brought me in to possess this land: but for the wickedness of these nations the LORD doth drive them out from before thee."* Deu. 9:3–4. But who cause these people to be wicked? Is it not God Himself? God said man's thoughts are in His hand—He turns it as He sees fit. The Bible says as a man thinks so is he. Earlier God revealed to us that it was Him who hardened Pharaoh's heart so that He might multiply His miracles. So who planned all of these events? It was no one but the One and only God. Did God create the previous inhabitants to cultivate the land for Israel before Israel's arrival? What has Israel done for God for Him to bless them in this magnitude? Nothing! *"For the LORD your God is God of gods, and Lord of lords, a great God, a mighty, and a terrible, which regardeth not persons, nor taketh reward."* Deu. 10:17. God's plan is likened unto an automobile manufacturing plant, the engineer who built the engine is as important as the one who built the body or the tires—because together, they build a vehicle. Individual built of itself has no value until it is combined with the rest of the other parts. So it is with the things of God. It doesn't matter who is being chosen to perform or execute what part of God's plan. Fulfilling your part is the only important thing for you.

The first inhabitants of the Promised Land were established by God; it was God Himself who afflicted them and drove them out of the land. The same God established Israel in this land to possess the land and dwell therein. This same God has revealed to Israel that their stay in this land may not be forever. It is this same God that shall bring it to pass the displacement of Israel in this land. John the Baptist was sent before Jesus to make the way; he completed his purpose. What was God's exit plan for John the Baptist? You think God did not have an exit plan for him? God's exit plan for John the Baptist was to be imprisoned and beheaded. Our Lord and Savior Jesus Christ was sent for mankind to be saved; He came and fulfilled His purpose. What was God's exit plan for Jesus? God's exit plan for Him was to die on the cross. Did Jesus or John commit any crime that they had to be killed? If you did not know of John, you may know of Jesus how He was to be killed—because it was written even before He came into being. Jesus said to the people witnessing His exit strategy that if it weren't for the power from God, they would not have succeeded in carrying out the plan. These plans are not your commonly called good plans—yet it was good that Jesus came and died for our sins.

The Acts of God

"See now that I, even I, am he, and there is no god with me: I kill, and I make alive; I wound, and I heal: neither is there any that can deliver out of my hand. For I lift up my hand to heaven, and say, I live for ever."

God is the God of everything. He is the God of the similar and the opposite: *"See now that I, even I, am he, and there is no god with me: I kill, and I make alive; I wound, and I heal: neither is there any that can deliver out of my hand. For I lift up my hand to heaven, and say, I live for ever. If I whet my glittering sword, and mine hand take hold on judgment; I will render vengeance to mine enemies, and will reward them that hate me. I will make mine arrows drunk with blood, and my sword shall devour flesh; and that with the blood of the slain and of the captives, from the beginning of revenges upon the enemy."* Deu.32:39–42.

From what we have seen, God established the first inhabitants of the Promised Land—well, that was a good thing! He then, drove them out—well, that was a bad thing right? Wrong! If God had not driven them out, Israel would not have been able to occupy. Make sense? The first inhabitants were supposed to be extinct to make the land vacant—well, that was ugly right? Wrong again! If they are not extinct, they may come back and claim ownership of the land. Now watch this with me; God established the Israelites after He had driven out the first inhabitants—well, that was not all that good is it? Did you see the complement? If you did not know anything about the first inhabitants, God's establishment of the Israelites in the Promised Land would have been a great thing. Now that you know God had to vacate one in order to accommodate another, your feeling is mixed. But wait, God said this same cycle that the first inhabitants experienced with the land could happen to Israel as well. Today Israel is facing suicide bombers and assassins in their midst—are these the pricks God was talking about? Today, there are nations surrounding Israel that believe Israel should not exist—are these the thorns God was talking about? You see, the acts of God come in various forms—the good, the bad, and the ugly are all the acts of God—which complement one another.

God of Everything

When Jonah fled from the presence of God (not knowing that God is everywhere), who sent the wind? *"But the LORD sent out a great wind into the sea, and there was a mighty tempest in the sea, so that the ship was like to be broken."* Jnh. 1:4. After knowing that they had a cursed one with them in the ship, the crew dealt with him. *"So they took up Jonah, and cast him forth into the sea: and the sea ceased from her raging."* Jnh. 1:15. Look at the great plan God had for Jonah and his journey; a fish swallowed Jonah and transported him to his destination at no cost: *"And the LORD spake unto the fish, and it vomited out Jonah upon the dry land."* Jnh. 2:10. Afterwards, Jonah went ahead and completed the assignment God had given him, from which he was running away.

Since man cannot defeat the purpose of God, it is left for man to obey and let the plan of God to take effect. We need to understand God; otherwise, we'll always be at war with God. When God proposed that Israel would inherit the land He promised their forefathers, it did indeed take long, and many lives were lost; however, the promise was fulfilled. *"And the LORD gave them rest round about, according to all that he sware unto their fathers: and there stood not a man of all their enemies before them; the LORD delivered all their enemies into their hand. There failed not ought of any good thing which the LORD had spoken unto the house of Israel; all came to pass."* Jos. 21:44–45. But God also told the Israelites that even though they're the victors today, it does not exclude them from being the victim tomorrow. *"Therefore it shall come to pass, that as all good things are come upon you, which the LORD your God promised you; so shall the LORD bring upon you all evil things, until he have destroyed you from off this good land which the LORD your God hath given you. When ye have transgressed the covenant of the LORD your God, which he commanded you, and have gone and served other gods, and bowed yourselves to them; then shall the anger of the LORD be kindled against you, and ye shall perish quickly from off the good land which he hath given unto you."* Jos. 23:15–16. Today, the remnants of the land which Israel has possessed have become the speck in the eyes of the Israelites as God has promised.

So after several victories with God, the table is now being turned on Israel. Remember when God said to the Israelites if they don't drive out all the inhabitants that He would do to them what He planned to do to the inhabitants? And did I not tell you that it is not possible for one to claim a land forever? It turns out that I was somewhat right. As it is today, so also it has been in the past. No one owns a place forever.

Regardless of what Israel did and the reasons why God turned against them, Israel is now on the losing side (in our understanding). Listen, it doesn't matter what you think—the cultivation of this planet will continue according to God's plan. It is time for Israel to have a taste of the other side. *"And the anger of the LORD was hot against Israel, and he delivered them into the hands of spoilers that spoiled them, and he sold them into the hands of their enemies round about, so that they could not any longer stand before their enemies. Whithersoever they went out, the hand of the LORD was against them for evil, as the LORD had said, and as the LORD had sworn unto them: and they were greatly distressed."* Jdg. 2:14–15. The Bible says that God is not a respecter of persons. God would use anyone for His plans either as a victor or as a victim. It is therefore necessary for us not to misunderstand the approach of God's plan with our weak thinking; whether you're a victor or a victim, rejoice because God has chosen you. Relax! It is only your rationale that makes you feel victim or victor. As far as God is concerned, you have completed your purpose. We must stop focusing on what Israel or someone did wrong or we would miss the message God is showing us. We tend to blame ourselves when things go wrong. It is about time mankind begins to understand God better and stop blaming one another.

Deliverance

Everyone wants to be delivered from one thing or the other, but how many people want to be delivered into the hands of an enemy or the destroyer? By exhibition of events in the Bible, we are going to explore this topic. What does it mean when the Bible says God delivered a person or persons into the hands of another? Wonder when one moment everything is going well with you and the next moment everything went in the wrong direction? This is it, the person or persons being delivered usually will face God's other side. God will change the thinking, seeing, hearing, thought process, strength, normal support, and other things that would have otherwise given that person(s) being delivered confidence and/or victory. To the person being delivered, this is wrath. However, to the person or persons at the receiving end of the delivery, this is victory. For example, this was the victory announcement for Israel against Jericho: *"But the LORD thy God shall deliver them unto thee, and shall destroy them with a mighty destruction, until they be destroyed. And he shall deliver their kings into thine hand, and thou shalt destroy their name from under heaven: there shall no man be able to stand before thee, until thou have destroyed them."* Deu. 7:23–24. This was not so much of a victory to the people of Jericho when they heard of the coming of Joshua and Israel. *"And as soon as we had heard these things, our hearts did melt, neither did there remain any more courage in any man, because of you: for the LORD your God, he is God in heaven above, and in earth beneath."* Jos. 2:11. Thus, Israel went forth and destroyed the city of Jericho *"And they utterly destroyed all that was in the city, both man and woman, young and old, and ox, and sheep, and ass, with the edge of the sword."* Jos. 6:21.

As it is evident with this event, it is not that God planned the victory outcome and Satan planned the losing outcome. It is God who planned both sides of the outcome.

Usually, Israel is comfortable with their enemies or is blinded into whom their enemies are; this is because nothing happens without God. It was usually when God delivered them into the hands of their enemies that Israel would realize these people were their enemies. So, was God revealing to the Israelites their enemies (those to destroy) when He delivered them into the hands of their enemies? By the way, these were the same people God said He would wipe out by little by little or for Israel to wipe them out of their sight. Also, they usually returned to God when He delivered them into the hands of their enemies. But the most important delivery I want to point out here is the one that relates to the Israelites and a mighty man named Samson.

Before Samson was born, God delivered the Israelites into the hands of the Philistines for forty years. His birth came to pass from a woman we would consider barren—being that she gave birth tells me that God did not consider her barren. It is only God that can make a woman barren until the appointed time—was Samson created for a specific purpose? Many women who were considered barren but who gave birth anyway usually gave birth to someone on a 'special mission' distinct to the human eye.

In the past God had not wanted the children of Israel to intermarry with their neighbors; this time, God wanted Samson to go and be married to a Philistine woman. Why? Because through Samson God wanted to destroy the Philistines to whom He had delivered Israel into captivity. *"But his father and his mother knew not that it was of the LORD, that he sought an occasion against the Philistines: for at that time the Philistines had dominion over Israel."* Jdg. 14:4. It used to be an abomination for the Israelites to get in marriage with the nations around them. Not this time; God wanted Samson to be married to a Philistine so that Samson could infiltrate into the Philistines and destroy them. The confusion between Samson and the Philistines began when the woman who was supposed to be Samson's wife was given to his friend for marriage. Do you think this is how God planned it to be? Yes and yes. Therefore Samson got very angry with the Philistines; he went and burned their farms, and they in turn burnt the woman and her father to death. Samson then avenged that killing with his own killing of a thousand Philistines and gained respect from the Philistines and judged Israel for twenty years. However, the Philistines pressed on and sought ways to kill Samson. And it came to pass that they plotted with his lover named Delilah and she found out the secret of his power and she removed it. *"And she said, The Philistines be upon thee, Samson. And he awoke out of his sleep, and said, I will go out as at other times before, and shake myself.* **And he wist not that the LORD was departed from him.** *But the Philistines took him, and put out his eyes, and brought him down to Gaza, and bound him with fetters of brass; and he did grind in the prison house."* Jdg. 16:20–21.

Although the Lord was with Samson when he defeated the Philistines, Samson himself was delivered to and died with the same Philistines whom the Lord deliberately delivered into his hands for destruction. *"Now the house was full of men and women; and all the lords of the Philistines were there; and there were upon the roof about three thousand men and women, that beheld while Samson made sport. And Samson called unto the LORD, and said, O Lord God, remember me, I pray thee, and strengthen me, I pray thee, only this once, O God, that I may be at once avenged of the Philistines for my two eyes. And Samson took hold of the two middle pillars upon which the house stood, and on which it was borne up, of the one with his right hand, and of the other with his left. And Samson said, Let me die with the Philistines. And he bowed himself with all his might; and the house fell upon the lords, and upon all the people that were therein. So the dead which he slew at his death were more than they which he slew in his life."* Jdg. 16:27–30. If you don't know why God left Samson, please don't tell me that Samson did something wrong and that's why God left him to be bound, lose his eyes, and subsequently die. The Spirit of God does not die with a man; the Spirit of God departed from the Lord Jesus before He gave up the ghost at Calvary. Did the Lord Jesus do anything wrong? No, but His mission had been completed; that is why the Spirit of God left him. If Samson was to use his life to avenge the Philistines, did God have to tell anyone before He did it? The fact of the matter is that God prepared Samson to defeat the Philistines even with his life. What is life if it does not fulfill what purpose God has for it? As God used the Philistines to destroy the Israelites and Samson, so also He used Samson to destroy the Philistines. As Samson was delivered to die, so also the Philistines were delivered to die—purpose fulfilled.

There is a song we commonly sing for comfort… "The Devil can't give it, and the Devil can't take it away." Here is the truth to that. It is God that gives it, and it is God that can take it away. Saul was crowned by God, and it is God that dethroned him. Although Samuel was dead at the time, Saul went and desperately invoked his spirit through a witch, and Samuel spoke to him: *"Moreover the LORD will also deliver Israel with thee into the hand of the Philistines: and to morrow shalt thou and thy sons be with me: the LORD also shall deliver the host of Israel into the hand of the Philistines."* 1 Sam. 28:19. When God said He would bring an end to Saul's reign, He was not kidding around. In one day, Saul and his sons were killed by the Philistines. *"And the Philistines followed hard upon Saul and upon his sons; and the Philistines slew Jonathan, and Abinadab, and Melchishua, Saul's sons. And the battle went sore against Saul, and the archers hit him; and he was sore wounded of the archers. Then said Saul unto his armourbearer, Draw thy sword, and thrust me through therewith; lest these uncircumcised come and thrust me through, and abuse me. But his armourbearer would not; for he was sore afraid. Therefore Saul took a sword, and fell upon it."* 1 Sam. 31:2–4. Not only were Saul and his sons killed, Israel was also humiliated. Saul's head was cut off and was displayed throughout the land of the Philistines and in the house of their idols to mock Israel. *"And they cut off his head, and stripped off his armour, and sent into the land of the Philistines round about, to publish it in the house of their idols, and among the people."* 1 Sam. 31:9. Thus God authored the rise and fall of Saul.

We have been trained to give credit to an enemy (Satan) that in reality is not even positioned to be able to receive credit.

When Israel was exiled to Assyria, was it the power of God that sent them to exile or the power of the king of Assyria? As you must have learned, the king of Assyria did not have any power except that which God had given to him. Therefore, it was not according to the power of the king of Assyria but the power of God which delivered them into the hands of their enemies. *"And the LORD rejected all the seed of Israel, and afflicted them, and delivered them into the hand of spoilers, until he had cast them out of his sight."* 2Ki. 17:20. This was how Israel was taken into exile by their spoilers as the Lord had said it. *"Surely at the commandment of the LORD came this upon Judah, to remove them out of his sight…"* 2Ki. 24:3. You have heard in the past that Israel was exiled because of sin; I'll also ask you, did God not know what Israel would do before it happened?

It was NOT the power of any enemies; it was the power of God—it may have been related to the sin of Israel, yet it was the power of God that sent them into exile, not the devil or enemy. *"But after that our fathers had provoked the God of heaven unto wrath, he gave them into the hand of Nebuchadnezzar the king of Babylon, the Chaldean, who destroyed this house, and carried the people away into Babylon."* Ezr. 5:12. We have been trained to give credit to an enemy (Satan) that in reality is not even positioned to be able to receive credit.

Let's dig deeper; when Israel was exiled to Assyria, I told you it was God that sent them off onto that path! This is what God said about Assyria in regards to their role in Israel's exile: *"O Assyrian, the rod of mine anger, and the staff in their hand is mine indignation. I will send him against an hypocritical nation, and against the people of my wrath will I give him a charge, to take the spoil, and to take the prey, and to tread them down like the mire of the streets."* Isa. 10:5–6. God said, as a man uses cane to flog his child so were the Assyrians to Him against Israel and the other nations the Assyrians afflicted with pain.

Job was described to be an upright and perfect man by God. When Satan was looking for work, God directed him to Job. Satan, as many of you well know, works as the Tester or Tempter for God's creations—he brings the bad reports. *"And the LORD said unto Satan, Hast thou considered my servant Job, that there is non like him in the earth, a perfect and an upright man, one that feareth God, and escheweth evil?"* Job 1:8. It was God that referred Satan to Job, and it was God Himself that delivered Job into the hands of Satan to be afflicted. *"And the LORD said unto Satan, Behold, all that he hath is in thy power; only opon himslef put not forth thine hand." Job 1:12.* In fact, digging deeper you'll see that it was God Himself who afflicted Job—Satan said to God, touch him and he'll curse you to your face, and God delivered Job into the hands of Satan. *"But put forth thine hand now, and touch his bone and his flesh, and he will curse thee to thy face. And the LORD said unto Satan, Behold, he is in thine hand; but save his life. So went Satan forth from the presence of the LORD, and smote Job with sore boils from the sole of his foot unto his crown."* Job 2:5–7. You mean even Satan advice God? No question! Notice that he came and also reported to God when the other angels came with their reports. Satan seems to behave as the one who seeks and bring bad reports. This is why he is called the Accuser. The million-dollar question is this: Is Satan also an angel of God? If no, then why are we not giving credit to Satan instead of God after we have gained our victory from his destruction? If yes, then why are we giving credit (credit? I mean blame) to Satan instead of God? Why blame the messenger? After Job had been afflicted from all ends and by all means, through the Sabeans, Chaldeans, Satan, earth, and heaven and had lost everything, Job said he knew who did all these: *"... the LORD gave, and the LORD hath taken away; blessed be the name of the LORD."* Job 1:21.

Did Satan go and tell the Sabeans and Chaldeans, thus said the God of heaven and earth, thou shall go and destroy all that Job has—I have delivered them unto you? What about the fire from God that consumed the sheep and servants—was that truly from God? What about the great wind from the wilderness that smote the house and killed all the children of Job—was that from God?

Satan is just the name of one angel as Gabriel is another angel.

Satan is just the name of one angel as Gabriel is another angel. I would ask you again, is Satan working for God or himself? Until this point, the name Satan had been used very rarely. The vivid function of Satan was revealed in this epic. Satan was classified as the tempter of man: a messenger of God—the Angel that tested man and brought the evil reports. The Angel that put new products into tryout and report on imperfect old products. The one who brought all types of trials and temptations to man. Satan is like modern-day quality assurance, commonly called QA. Satan is a messenger of God who reports back to God. For this reasons, if you give blame to Satan, you've denied God the credit.

For those of you who do not know God as the Almighty, what do you need to happen to you before you accept that He is the Almighty? Nebuchadnezzar, the king of Assyria who sent Israel to exile, came to learn in a very hard way that there was an Almighty God and that nothing happened without God. He was almost turned into an eagle before he acknowledged or came to know that God was the most high. *"And they shall drive thee from men, and thy dwelling shall be with the beasts of the field: they shall make thee to eat grass as oxen, and seven times shall pass over thee, until thou know that the most High ruleth in the kingdom of men, and giveth it to whomsoever he will. The same hour was the thing fulfilled upon Nebuchadnezzar: and he was driven from men, and did eat grass as oxen, and his body was wet with the dew of heaven, till his hairs were grown like eagles' feathers, and his nails like birds' claws."* Dan. 4:32–33. After being humbled in this manner, Nebuchadnezzar testified and proclaimed that there was a mighty God. Furthermore, he testified that there was nothing that happened without God *"And all the inhabitants of the earth are reputed as nothing: and he doeth according to his will in the army of heaven, and among the inhabitants of the earth: and none can stay his hand, or say unto him, What doest thou?"* Dan. 4:35.

Desire

Many have frequently argued blindly that it is through one's evil desire that Satan can use them for evil purpose. Only few would argue correctly that it is God that creates and decides the purpose of each creation. While the first was true in the past, it is no longer true since we have gained better understanding of the things of God.

During the time of Solomon king of Israel, Solomon was a man of great love and romance without boundaries; he fell in love with women from nations whom God commanded the Israelites not to intermarry. These women caused Solomon to stray from the commandments of God, so God declared that He would take away the kingdom from him. To begin the breakup of the kingdom from Solomon and his descendants, God started by stirring up adversaries for Solomon.

Now, to remove the ignorance in many regarding the creation and purpose of every being, let's examine the distressful events of Solomon until his death. As you read further, note, it was not the evil desires of the people mentioned that resulted the downfall of Solomon. *"And the LORD stirred up an adversary unto Solomon, Hadad the Edomite: he was of the king's seed in Edom."* 1Ki. 11:14. What does this tell you? That it was not the evil desires of Hadad that made him Solomon's adversary. It was because that was God's purpose for Hadad (Hadad was a boy during the time of King David; he escaped to Egypt when David slew the Edomites). Did Hadad fulfilled his God-given purpose? Yes!

The purpose of every being is defined in the plan God has for them.

Though God intended to take the kingdom away from Solomon, He planned to take it away not during Solomon's time, but during the time of his son. So Solomon was distressed by Hadad during his apportioned time. *"And God stirred him up another adversary, Rezon the son of Eliadah, which fled from his lord Hadadezer king of Zobah:"* 1Ki. 11:23.

Very rarely you will find that a people God marked for destruction successfully escaped. But because these people were destined for other purpose of God, they were preserved and their escape was a success. Nothing escapes from God! The purpose of every being is defined in the plan God has for them. Even some of Solomon's loyalists rose up against him and became his adversaries. *"And Jeroboam the son of Nebat, an Ephrathite of Zereda, Solomon's servant, whose mother's name was Zeruah, a widow woman, even he lifted up his hand against the king."* 1Ki. 11:26. These were Solomon's last days as king of Israel until his death. His adversaries were sent by God not because of their evil desires.

After the death of Solomon, God split the kingdom out of the hand of Solomon; out of this kingdom Judah and Israel were formed. Were the division of Israel by the foes of Solomon premeditated by those executing the plan or by God? *"…for the cause was from the LORD, that he might perform his saying, which the LORD spake by Ahijah the Shilonite unto Jeroboam the son of Nebat."* 1Ki. 12:15. This shakeup of Israel during the time of Solomon was just the beginning of what God had planned. As it was later revealed, those who were put in place to head both Judah and Israel were temporary. They were, however, removed from their posts with charges and justification in anticipation of the great King. Thus God communicated with them in those days.

Examine for what it's worth this case of a lion and a man of God. *"And when he was gone, a lion met him by the way, and slew him: and his carcase was cast in the way, and the ass stood by it, the lion also stood by the carcase."* 1Ki. 13:24. God intended that the man of God be killed and his body not buried in his family burial ground. It was neither the plan nor the desire of the lion to kill the man of God but God's plan. *"And when the prophet that brought him back from the way heard thereof, he said, It is the man of God, who was disobedient unto the word of the LORD: therefore the LORD hath delivered him unto the lion, which hath torn him, and slain him, according to the word of the LORD, which he spake unto him."* 1Ki. 13:26. After all, what desire does a lion has that it would kill a man and not consume it or to have an ass standing with it and not kill and eat it? This was a desire and plan of God. We need to stop the habit of saying it is one's desire that leads them to do evil—because we simply don't know.

Without the plan and approval from God, nothing happens. David knew this, and he did not hesitate to enquire from God time and time again before doing anything. As a result, God called David a man after His own heart. *"Then David enquired of the LORD yet again. And the LORD answered him and said, Arise, go down to Keilah; for I will deliver the Philistines into thine hand. So David and his men went to Keilah, and fought with the Philistines, and brought away their cattle, and smote them with a great slaughter. So David saved the inhabitants of Keilah."* 1 Sam. 23:4–5. But for Saul, who sought to kill David, God did not deliver David into the hands of Saul, and therefore Saul was unsuccessful. *"And David abode in the wilderness in strong holds, and remained in a mountain in the wilderness of Ziph. And Saul sought him every day, but God delivered him not into his hand."* 1 Sam. 23:14. Again, it is God who can make anything happen. This time with much emphasis God assured David about the plan. *"And David enquired of the LORD, saying, Shall I go up to the Philistines? wilt thou deliver them into mine hand? And the LORD said unto David, Go up: for I will **doubtless deliver the Philistines into thine hand**."* 2 Sam. 5:9. And with great success did David smite the Philistines.

If it is at all man's fault because of sin, still it is God through whom the good, bad, evil, and dismay come. God said He gave man statutes that man cannot overcome, and in the gift (blessing) He polluted man. *"Wherefore I gave them also statutes that were not good, and judgments whereby they should not live; And I polluted them in their own gifts, in that they caused to pass through the fire all that openeth the womb, that I might make them desolate, to the end that they might know that I am the LORD."* Eze. 20:25–26.

Jesus testified in His prayer about how God planned everything according to His eternal purpose. *"And he went a little farther, and fell on his face, and prayed, saying, O my Father, if it be possible, let this cup pass from me: nevertheless not as I will, but as thou wilt."* Mt. 26:39. Jesus said—**"nevertheless not as I will, but as thou wilt."** That is, not as He desired, but as God desires. Whose will? In your opinion and understanding, is this will a good or a bad will? The will of God came to pass as Jesus humbly requested His crucifixion. Many had agreed that the greatest gift from God to mankind besides life was this will—His grace—the love of God that brought Jesus to die for our sins. The will of God comes in various forms. The crucifixion is a perfect and good will for which Jesus our Lord and Savior came. And if you have not realized that, I recommend you start thinking about how you can understand the will and ways of God—pick up a Bible and get started—find yourself a Bible-based church.

The Acts of God

"Shall there be evil in a city, and the LORD hath not done it?"

"Shall a trumpet be blown in the city, and the people not be afraid? Shall there be evil in a city, and the LORD hath not done it?" Am. 3:6.

"And also I have withholden the rain from you, when there were yet three months to the harvest: and I caused it to rain upon one city, and caused it not to rain upon another city: one piece was rained upon, and the piece whereupon it rained not withered." Am. 4:7.

"I have sent among you the pestilence after the manner of Egypt: your young men have I slain with the sword, and have taken away your horses; and I have made the stink of your camps to come up unto your nostrils: yet have ye not returned unto me, saith the LORD." Am. 4:10.

"I have overthrown some of you, as God overthrew Sodom and Gomorrah, and ye were as a firebrand plucked out of the burning: yet have ye not returned unto me, saith the LORD." Am. 4:11.

"Behold, the days come, saith the Lord GOD, that I will send a famine in the land, not a famine of bread, nor a thirst for water, but of hearing the words of the LORD: And they shall wander from sea to sea, and from the north even to the east, they shall run to and fro to seek the word of the LORD, and shall not find it." Am. 8:11–12.

I hope that all these events mentioned throughout this chapter has helped you to understand the power and authority behind every event. Get rid of the understanding that someone somewhere share these qualities with God. All power and authority belong to God and He had discharged them according to His eternal purpose. We may not find the value and purpose of some events now; however, at the proper time they would be apparent. God had established all laws according to their functions. A long time ago, force of gravity was considered bad until someone understood the importance of it. God is the cause of everything that had been and is to be.

Questions to Ponder

Do humans have the ability to change God's purpose?

What is God's will in your life, and what do you intend to do about it?

CHAPTER THREE

HE CAUSES ALL THINGS—THE JOSEPH STORY

Fundamentals:

"And he dreamed yet another dream, and told it his brethren, and said, Behold, I have dreamed a dream more; and, behold, the sun and the moon and the eleven stars made obeisance to me." Gen. 37:9.

"And the Midianites sold him into Egypt unto Potiphar, an officer of Pharaoh's, and captain of the guard." Gen. 37:36.

"And Joseph was the governor over the land, and he it was that sold to all the people of the land: and Joseph's brethren came, and bowed down themselves before him with their faces to the earth." Gen. 42:6.

Let's take a closer look at the idea that God causes all things, using the story of Joseph as an example. The story of Joseph depicts how we human beings can easily see the plans of God being flawed. It is a story that when I read it, I very often get emotional—not only about the things that Joseph went through for God's divine plan to manifest, but moreso over the fact that people today are not able to understand this message and how God works, and that people continue to talk about this story in a manner that is unfruitful. People say that the brothers were bad-tempered, Joseph should have kept his mouth shut about his dream, the enemy (what enemy?) planned evil against

Joseph but God turned it around to be good, and many other such statements. For those of you who are not familiar with the story of Joseph, I promise you won't be left out. In this chapter, we're going to recreate and dissect the story of Joseph so that you can see how God works and how we very often misunderstand the ways of God. After reading this Joseph's story, when you are afflicted or troubled, put on your dancing shoes and rejoice; because God is taking you somewhere He has planned.

God's Perfect Plan for Joseph

And it came to pass in a certain night that God revealed to Joseph in a dream what he would become. And Joseph told it to his brothers, for he had eleven brothers:

"For, behold, we were binding sheaves in the field, and, lo, my sheaf arose, and also stood upright; and, behold, your sheaves stood round about, and made obeisance to my sheaf." Gen. 37:7.

"And he dreamed yet another dream, and told it his brethren, and said, Behold, I have dreamed a dream more; and, behold, the sun and the moon and the eleven stars made obeisance to me." Gen. 37:9. When Joseph told his brothers his dreams, they hated him. After all, he was their younger brother; who was he to tell them that they'd serve him and bow down to him? With our human understanding, I am sure when God revealed to Joseph that he'd become a great leader, Joseph must have asked, "How is this possible when I am only a boy and one of the least among my brothers?" But first, let me introduce you into the plan God had prepared for Joseph—God's will for Joseph:

Joseph, My will for you is to become a great leader. However, this is how it will manifest: Your brothers will hate you because your father loves you so much. Out of this hatred, they'll sell you to the Midianites. The Midianites will sell you as a slave to an Egyptian named Potiphar. However, Potiphar is an officer of Pharaoh the king of Egypt. You will find grace with Potiphar, and though you will be thrown into prison, even in that prison, you will find grace with the keeper of the prison. Do not worry about your location, because your good work at this time will reveal and introduce you to Pharaoh, the king of Egypt. Pharaoh will find you to be so good that he will make you his second in command; even Pharaoh, will subject himself to your judgment. And during this time, you will save the lives of many, even your brothers who hated you and sold you. And yes, they will bow down to you. Joseph, do not worry about your brothers' behavior towards you. For this is My great plan.

If God had revealed the plan to Joseph this way, certainly everyone would be in a queue to know God's plan for their lives. People would be willing to be included in God's plan. But no, that is not how God revealed it to him, and God has not changed the way He makes His plan known to mankind. As we'll see, Joseph went through pain and afflictions; yet, it was ALL PART of God's plan.

The Dialogue between God and Joseph

Let's go into a simulated conversation God had with Joseph and the journey of Joseph into his destiny—the will of God.

God: Joseph, I have made a plan for you so that you'll become a great leader and you will save your family and many from death during an upcoming famine. I will make you a leader even in that great kingdom Egypt. Even your older brothers and your little brother Benjamin, and the sun, and the moon will bow down to you in your greatness.

Joseph: How can I become a leader in Egypt and a savior to my family and to many? This is not possible. I don't even know where Egypt is located on the map. Besides, in our custom it is the oldest child that inherits and becomes the leader of the family; I am almost the least among my brothers.

God: Joseph, it does not matter who is the oldest in the family. What matters is whom I have chosen. Also, you do not need to know where Egypt is; I have made plans for you regarding your trip to Egypt. Furthermore, I will make all the provisions you'll need to make sure your judgment is right and you'll do all that is necessary to save lives including your family during the famine.

Joseph: My brothers hate me too much for me to succeed in this plan. Please give it to someone else; otherwise my brothers will kill me because of this plan.

God: That's all right Joseph; I will cause your brothers to help you in your journey to that great

If they don't hate you, they can't help you.

kingdom, and they will not even know that they're helping you fulfill that which they have hated you for. I want you to count it all joy when your brothers continue to hate you, because their hatred towards you will cause them to help you fulfill what I have planned for you. If they don't hate you, they can't help you.

Joseph: I don't even have money to go to Egypt. My father would not approve this plan and give me money for my fare.

God: It is for this reason and purpose I have created you. Therefore, neither I nor you need approval from your father. Your father himself will also help you in this plan. By the way, your journey is at hand. Your fare is on Me. Behold, I am with you always.

"And Israel said unto Joseph, Do not thy brethren feed the flock in Shechem? come, and I will send thee unto them. And he said to him, Here am I. And he said to him, Go, I pray thee, see whether it be well with thy brethren, and well with the flocks; and bring me word again. So he sent him out of the vale of Hebron, and he came to Shechem." Gen. 37:13–14.

Meanwhile his brothers were headed to Dothan, so Joseph journeyed towards Dothan. "And when they saw him afar off, even before he came near unto them, they conspired against him to slay him. And they said one to another, Behold, this dreamer cometh." Gen. 37:18–19.

"And Judah said unto his brethren, What profit is it if we slay our brother, and conceal his blood? Come, and let us sell him to the Ishmeelites, and let not our hand be upon him; for he is our brother and our flesh. And his brethren were content. Then there passed by Midianites merchantmen; and they drew and lifted up Joseph out of *the pit, and sold Joseph to the Ishmeelites for twenty pieces of silver: and they brought Joseph into Egypt."* Gen. 37:26–28.

"And the Midianites sold him into Egypt unto Potiphar, an officer of Pharaoh's, and captain of the guard." Gen. 37:36.

God: *Did I not tell you not to worry about how you'd get to Egypt and your fare? Welcome to Egypt!*

Joseph: *Welcome to Egypt? I have been sold by my brothers, and now I am a slave in Egypt. How can I be my father's favorite son and yet end up becoming a slave in a foreign land, and You say welcome to Egypt? This plan is absolutely ridiculous and unacceptable—it stinks.*

God: *Do not despise your small beginning. You'll become the best slave Egypt has ever known.*

And Joseph found grace in the sight of his master Potiphar, who made Joseph overseer of his household. So Joseph prospered as a slave in the house of his master.

And it came to pass that Joseph was imprisoned due to an allegation made by his master's wife (who didn't know she was helping him). Certainly, Joseph was furious with God as to why He let him out of his comfort zone even to the point of being in prison for a crime he did not commit.

Joseph: *Why am I now in prison in this Your so-called plan?*

God: *Count it all joy. You'll become the best prisoner Egypt has ever known. I will not change the plans I have for you. Therefore, do not despise your small beginning. It is the path for your greatness.*

Joseph: *What type of plan is this that I have to be in prison to become a great leader?*

God: *Joseph, do not focus on your environment. I am with you even in prison. You'll find favor in this prison and be liked by everyone. Everything in this prison will be kept in your care because of My favor and mercy in you. Everything you do, I'll make it prosper.*

Joseph: *I don't want to be a leader in a prison. What type of leader is this?*

God: *The prison is included in your path to introduce you to Pharaoh and his kingdom. Did you notice that you were not just placed in any prison but the prison where Pharaoh's prisoners are kept? Would you have preferred if I had introduced you to Pharaoh from Canaan?*

Would you have preferred if I had asked you to move to Egypt from Canaan by yourself? You didn't even know where Egypt was; you had nothing, not even your transportation fare. When you were a slave, did you lack anything or were you treated badly? While you're in prison, have you lacked or have you been treated badly? I want you to stop focusing on names people are calling you and the things that surround you. When you have become that great leader I have planned for you to be, do not focus on the environment and names people will be calling you, because you'll lose focus on what I have called you to do. My plan for you is perfect and genuine. All that you've learned while a slave and in prison will be useful to you when you become that great leader. Is it not only God that interprets dreams? Did I not reveal to you the interpretations of those dreams from the servants of Pharaoh? Did not the chief butler say he'll remember you when he's restored to his post? He'll remember you at the appointed time; he'll not remember you too soon, nor will he remember you too late.

Joseph Promoted from Slave to Ruler

"And it came to pass at the end of two full years, that Pharaoh dreamed: and, behold, he stood by the river… And it came to pass in the morning that his spirit was troubled; and he sent and called for all the magicians of Egypt, and all the wise men thereof: and Pharaoh told them his dream; but there was none that could interpret them unto Pharaoh. Then spake the chief butler unto Pharaoh, saying,…And there was there with us a young man, an Hebrew, servant to the captain of the guard; and we told him, and he interpreted to us our dreams; to each man according to his dream he did interpret. And it came to pass, as he interpreted to us, so it was; me he restored unto mine office, and him he hanged. Then Pharaoh sent and called Joseph, and they brought him hastily out of the dungeon: and he shaved himself, and changed his raiment, and came in unto Pharaoh. And Pharaoh said unto Joseph, I have dreamed a dream, and there is none that can interpret it: and I have heard say of thee, that thou canst understand a dream to interpret it. And Joseph answered Pharaoh, saying, It is not in me: God shall give Pharaoh an answer of peace. And Pharaoh said unto Joseph, In my dream, behold, I stood upon the bank of the river: And, behold, *there came up out of the river seven kine, fatfleshed and well favoured; and they fed in a meadow: And, behold, seven other kine came up after them, poor and very ill favoured and leanfleshed, such as I never saw in all the land of Egypt for badness: And the lean and the ill favoured kine did eat up the first seven fat kine: And when they had eaten them up, it could not be known that they had eaten them; but they were still ill favoured, as at the beginning. So I awoke. And I saw in my dream, and, behold, seven ears came up in one stalk, full and good: And, behold, seven ears, withered, thin, and blasted with the east wind, sprung up after them: And the thin ears devoured the seven good ears: and I told this unto the magicians; but there was none that could declare it to me. And Joseph said unto Pharaoh, The dream of Pharaoh is one: God hath shewed Pharaoh what he is about to do. The seven good kine are seven years; and the seven good ears are seven years: the dream is one. And the seven thin and ill favoured kine that came up after them are seven years; and the seven empty ears blasted with the east wind shall be seven years of famine. This is the thing which I have spoken unto Pharaoh: What God is about to do he sheweth unto Pharaoh. Behold, there come seven years of great plenty throughout all the land of Egypt: And there shall arise after them seven years of famine; and all the plenty shall be forgotten in the land of Egypt; and the famine shall consume the land; And the plenty shall not be known in the land by reason of that famine following; for it shall be very grievous. And for that the dream was doubled unto Pharaoh twice; it is because the thing is established by God, and God will shortly bring it to pass. Now therefore let Pharaoh look out a man discreet and wise, and set him over the land of Egypt. Let Pharaoh do this, and let him appoint officers over the land, and take up the fifth part of the land of Egypt in the seven plenteous years. And let them gather all the food of those good years that come, and lay up corn under the hand of Pharaoh, and let them keep food in the cities. And that food shall be for store to the land against the seven years of famine, which shall be in the land of Egypt; that the land perish not through the famine. And the thing was good in the eyes of Pharaoh, and in the eyes of all his servants. And Pharaoh said unto his servants, Can we find such a one as this is, a man in whom the Spirit of God is? And Pharaoh said unto Joseph, Forasmuch as God hath shewed thee all this,* there is none so discreet and wise as thou art: **Thou shalt be over my house, and according unto thy word shall all my people be ruled**: only in the throne will I be greater than thou. And Pharaoh said unto Joseph, See, I have set thee over all the land of Egypt. And Pharaoh took off his ring from his hand, and put it upon Joseph's hand, and arrayed him in vestures of fine linen, and put a gold chain about his neck; And he made him to ride in the second chariot which he had; and they cried before him, Bow the knee: **and he made him ruler over all the land of Egypt**." Gen.41:1–43.

Now, had God fulfilled His plan for Joseph? The answer is a yes just in case you missed it. Joseph has become a great leader. Wait a minute—God had not reunited him with his father and brothers yet. Joseph was sold when he was seventeen years old. He is now thirty years old and a leader; would his father recognize him if he were to see him? Does his father still live? Would his brothers recognize him if they were to see him? How were they doing? Let's keep going...

The Great Famine from God

And the seven years of plenty came, and Joseph and Egypt gathered and stored as Joseph had interpreted for Pharaoh. And the seven years of famine also came, and Joseph sold from the storehouses to the Egyptians and also to all the people that came from other countries to buy corn in Egypt, because the famine spread throughout the region including Canaan. It was among these people from other countries that Joseph recognized his brothers. However his brothers did not recognize him, and he did not make himself known to them.

"And Joseph was the governor over the land, and he it was that sold to all the people of the land: and Joseph's brethren came, and bowed down themselves before him with their faces to the earth." Gen. 42:6.

Then, Joseph seized the moment and decided to create chaos among his brothers by saying that they were spies. They denied that they were spies and indicated that they were brothers of twelve, the youngest with their father at home and the other no more, Joseph demanded that they bring their youngest brother from home to prove their innocence of spying. Joseph did this by detaining one of the brothers while he sent the rest to go and bring their youngest brother. And his brothers murmured among themselves why this had come upon them.

"And they said one to another, We are verily guilty concerning our brother, in that we saw the anguish of his soul, when he besought us, and we would not hear; therefore is this distress come upon us. And Reuben answered them, saying, Spake I not unto you, saying, Do not sin against the child; and ye would not hear? therefore, behold, also his blood is required. And they knew not that Joseph understood them; for he spake unto them by an interpreter. And he turned himself about from them, and wept; and returned to them again, and communed with them, and took from them Simeon, and bound him before their eyes." Gen. 42:21–24.

So the brethren journeyed back to Canaan… *"And they came unto Jacob their father unto the land of Canaan, and told him all that befell unto them; saying, The man, who is the lord of the land, spake roughly to us, and took us for spies of the country. And we said unto him, We are true men; we are no spies: We be twelve brethren, sons of our father; one is not, and the youngest is this day with our father in the land of Canaan. And the man, the lord of the country, said unto us, Hereby shall I know that ye are true men; leave one of your brethren here with me, and take food for the famine of your households, and be gone: And bring your youngest brother unto me: then shall I know that ye are no spies, but that ye are true men: so will I deliver you your brother, and ye shall traffick in the land."* Gen. 42:29–34.

After Jacob had refused many days to let his sons take Benjamin to Egypt to prove that they were not spies, he yielded to their demand and let them go when they had eaten up the food which they brought from Egypt during their first visit.

"Take also your brother, and arise, go again unto the man: And God Almighty give you mercy before the man, that he may send away your other brother, and Benjamin. If I be bereaved of my children, I am bereaved." Gen. 43:13–14.

"And when Joseph saw Benjamin with them, he said to the ruler of his house, Bring these men home, and slay, and make ready; for these men shall dine with me at noon. And the man did as Joseph bade; and

the man brought the men into Joseph's house. And the men were afraid, because they were brought into Joseph's house; and they said, Because of the money that was returned in our sacks at the first time are we brought in; that he may seek occasion against us, and fall upon us, and take us for bondmen, and our asses. And they came near to the steward of Joseph's house, and they communed with him at the door of the house, And said, O sir, we came indeed down at the first time to buy food: And it came to pass, when we came to the inn, that we opened our sacks, and, behold, every man's money was in the mouth of his sack, our money in full weight: and we have brought it again in our hand. And other money have we brought down in our hands to buy food: we cannot tell who put our money in our sacks. And he said, Peace be to you, fear not: your God, and the God of your father, hath given you treasure in your sacks: I had your money. And he brought Simeon out unto them. And the man brought the men into Joseph's house, and gave them water, and they washed their feet; and he gave their asses provender. And they made ready the present against Joseph came at noon: for they heard that they should eat bread there. And when Joseph came home, they brought him the present which was in their hand into the house, and bowed themselves to him to the earth. And he asked them of their welfare, and said, Is your father well, the old man of whom ye spake? Is he yet alive? And they answered, Thy servant our father is in good health, he is yet alive. And they bowed down their heads, and made obeisance. And he lifted up his eyes, and saw his brother Benjamin, his mother's son, and said, Is this your younger brother, of whom ye spake unto me? And he said, God be gracious unto thee, my son. And Joseph made haste; for his bowels did yearn upon his brother: and he sought where to weep; and he entered into his chamber, and wept there. And he washed his face, and went out, and refrained himself, and said, Set on bread. And they set on for him by himself, and for them by themselves, and for the Egyptians, which did eat with him, by themselves: because the Egyptians might not eat bread with the Hebrews; for that is an abomination unto the Egyptians. And they sat before him, the firstborn according to his birthright, and the youngest according to his youth: and the men marvelled one at another. And he took and sent messes unto them from before him: but Benjamin's mess was five times so much as any of their's. And they drank, and were merry with him." Gen. 43:16–34.

Chaos in Transit

And Joseph commanded his steward to make preparations for his brothers to return to Canaan with sacks of food. Although Joseph did not make himself known to his brothers when he sent them away, he did not plan for them to go far. Joseph conspired with his steward to put into each of his brothers' sacks the money they'd paid for the food they came to buy; in addition he had the steward put Joseph's silver cup into their younger brother Benjamin's sack. As the brothers headed to Canaan, Joseph ordered his steward to intercept his brothers and put a halt to their journey—in fact, bring them back. Talking about a chaotic situation turning into extreme chaos! On the way, they were overtaken by Joseph's men and were accused of paying evil for good—stealing a silver cup from the man who had treated them well: Joseph. They denied knowing anything about a silver cup and were searched. Before they were searched, not knowing what was in their sacks, they swore that if such a cup was found from any one of them, that person would die and the rest of them would be taken as bondmen. As they were searched, the cup was uncovered in Benjamin's sack, and it became evident that all of them were going back to Egypt as bondmen—including Benjamin, whom their father loved dearly.

"And Joseph said unto them, What deed is this that ye have done? wot ye not that such a man as I can certainly divine? And Judah said, What shall we say unto my lord? what shall we speak? or how shall we clear ourselves? God hath found out the iniquity of thy servants: behold, we are my lord's servants, both we, and he also with whom the cup is found. And he said, God forbid that I should do so: but the man in whose hand the cup is found, he shall be my servant; and as for you, get you up in peace unto your father. Then Judah came near unto him, and said, Oh my lord, let thy servant, I pray thee, speak a word in my lord's ears, and let not thine anger burn against thy servant: for thou art even as Pharaoh. My lord asked his servants, saying, Have ye a father, or

a brother? And we said unto my lord, We have a father, an old man, and a child of his old age, a little one; and his brother is dead, and he alone is left of his mother, and his father loveth him. And thou saidst unto thy servants, Bring him down unto me, that I may set mine eyes upon him. And we said unto my lord, The lad cannot leave his father: for if he should leave his father, his father would die. And thou saidst unto thy servants, Except your youngest brother come down with you, ye shall see my face no more. And it came to pass when we came up unto thy servant my father, we told him the words of my lord." Gen. 44:15–24.

Judah continued to plead with Joseph that he had placed himself as surety for Benjamin before their father and how their father's life would come to an end in sorrow if Benjamin was not returned to their father. *"Now therefore, I pray thee, let thy servant abide instead of the lad a bondman to my lord; and let the lad go up with his brethren. For how shall I go up to my father, and the lad be not with me? lest peradventure I see the evil that shall come on my father."* Gen. 44:33–34.

God Sent

When Joseph could not bear the plea any longer, he cried aloud and dismissed everyone with them. And with a crying voice he said unto his brothers, *"...**I am Joseph**; doth my father yet live?"* Gen. 45:3. And while his brothers were terrified and could not answer him nor comprehend what was

*"I am Joseph your brother, whom ye sold into Egypt. Now therefore be not grieved, nor angry with yourselves, that ye sold me hither: **for God did send me before you to preserve life.**"*

happening before them all, Joseph called them to himself and said, *"...I am Joseph your brother, whom ye sold into Egypt. Now therefore be not grieved, nor angry with yourselves, that ye sold me hither: **for God did send me before you to preserve life**. For these two years hath the famine been in the land: and yet there are five years, in the* *which there shall neither be earing nor harvest. And God sent me before you to preserve you a posterity in the earth, and to save your lives by a great deliverance. So now it was not you that sent me hither, but God: and he hath made me a father to Pharaoh, and lord of all his house, and a ruler throughout all the land of Egypt. Haste ye, and go up to my father, and say unto him, Thus saith thy son Joseph, God hath made me lord of all Egypt: come down unto me, tarry not: And thou shalt dwell in the land of Goshen, and thou shalt be near unto me, thou, and thy children, and thy children's children, and thy flocks, and thy herds, and all that thou hast: And there will I nourish thee; for yet there are five years of famine; lest thou, and thy household, and all that thou hast, come to poverty. And, behold, your eyes see, and the eyes of my brother Benjamin, that it is my mouth that speaketh unto you. And ye shall tell my father of all my glory in Egypt, and of all that ye have seen; and ye shall haste and bring down my father hither. And he fell upon his brother Benjamin's neck, and wept; and Benjamin wept upon his neck. Moreover he kissed all his brethren, and wept upon them: and after that his brethren talked with him."* Gen. 45:4–15.

Now when Pharaoh heard about the existing brothers of Joseph, he was pleased and did not waste any time in blessing them. Pharaoh commanded Joseph to stock their carriage with food and asked them to go to the land of Canaan and bring their father and the rest of their households so that they might enjoy and eat from the abundance of Egypt and not die from the famine. Additionally, Pharaoh also requested Joseph to send them away with extra wagons so as to bring their father and the rest of their households—and not to worry about their belongings in Canaan—for the good of Egypt was theirs. Joseph did as Pharaoh ordered and sent his brothers away. As they arrived back to Canaan and told their father all that has happened and that Joseph was yet alive, he could not believe it. Finally, after Jacob had heard Joseph's message word for word, and had seen the entourage that was sent for him, he believed. So Jacob (also called Israel) journeyed to Egypt with his household and did not fall victim to the seven years of famine.

The God of Multiplicity

At the time that Israel the nation went into Egypt, Israel was a total of seventy persons including Joseph and his two sons who were in Egypt already but excluding Israel's sons' wives. It was out of these seventy people that mankind experienced the greatest exodus: when Israel finally left Egypt, they were on the face of the earth like sand on the seashore—their population had grown from seventy to over six hundred thousand men aged twenty and older, besides women and children. This population growth occurred in 430 years—they overstayed their visa.

Now you know how the Israelites landed in Egypt. However, the core message is this: God made a plan for Joseph's life that had both upside and downside (based on our human understanding). The story was recorded particularly for us today so that we may learn and understand how God works and operate. Today, people are still looking at this story with the same level of ignorance as the people that were before them. The story was laid out so that we may through it understand God better. Was there any mistake in the plan God made for Joseph? As Joseph rightfully said to his brothers, "You thought to harm me, but God intended it for good." What Joseph was telling his brothers was that, in their human understanding, they were harming him; however, that was not what it was all about – they were helping him fulfill his purpose, because God had planned it even before they hated him and God's plans are always good. God made this plan from beginning to end including those hateful thoughts of Joseph's brothers. Out of those hateful thoughts, his brothers were able to execute their part of the plan God had made. Though hate is classified as a bad habit in our understanding, what stimulates someone into action is always rooted from the mind. That being said, God knew with hatred in the minds of Joseph's brothers they would be stimulated to sell Joseph and set him off in the path to Egypt—which is the destination for God's plan in his life. What you should always keep in mind is that the plan of God always

> *The outcome of the word 'thought' is based on the understanding of the person having the thought.*

supersedes the thoughts and thinking of human. The outcome of the word 'thought' is based on the understanding of the person having the thought. That thought does not and will never precede or supersede the plan and purpose of God. Read the complete story of Joseph in Genesis and see for yourself what I have seen. God's plans may seem imperfect at times to the human eye; however, do not be confused with what your eyes may see. The plans of God are flawless.

Questions to Ponder

Was there any flaw in the plan of Joseph's life?

What has God planned for your life?

Chapter Four

He Curses

Fundamentals:

"And the LORD God said unto the serpent, Because thou hast done this, thou art cursed above all cattle, and above every beast of the field; upon thy belly shalt thou go, and dust shalt thou eat all the days of thy life: And I will put enmity between thee and the woman, and between thy seed and her seed; it shall bruise thy head, and thou shalt bruise his heel. Unto the woman he said, I will greatly multiply thy sorrow and thy conception; in sorrow thou shalt bring forth children; and thy desire shall be to thy husband, and he shall rule over thee. And unto Adam he said, Because thou hast hearkened unto the voice of thy wife, and hast eaten of the tree, of which I commanded thee, saying, Thou shalt not eat of it: cursed is the ground for thy sake; in sorrow shalt thou eat of it all the days of thy life; Thorns also and thistles shall it bring forth to thee; and thou shalt eat the herb of the field; In the sweat of thy face shalt thou eat bread, till thou return unto the ground; for out of it wast thou taken: for dust thou art, and unto dust shalt thou return." Gen. 3:14–19.

The chaotic scene in the beginning—was this the plan of God? Sounds like hardware and/or software glitches at the beginning—parts not working together, applications not communicating during initial launching. We have learned that after God created the beasts and man, He then created the woman. The woman who was created to help the man happened to have an unexpected (or maybe not) functionality: disobedience. But does anything happen that God did not plan? If

God did not plan it, why then did it happen? Are we saying that things can happen without God?

We have established already that God knows the future and that nothing happens without Him. If that is the case, why did God allow the straying of man to be part of the creation? If God knew that the woman would not be compatible with the beast (animal), why then did He put them together in the same place? This is why I say that we need to seek understanding: because once this is gained, the purpose for the plan is revealed and the concept of something being the fault of one person or another is thrown away. This is part of God's plan for creation; man was created to cultivate the earth. The creation was not that God said He would create man and after creating man, if man turned left He would do option A and if man turned right He would do option B. That's not it! God was certain in the creation that He had made, and He said it was good.

In this chapter, we are going to exploit the topic of curse—does God curse? You may have heard a yes and a no answer to this very question. Who is correct and who is wrong? It depends—on the understanding in which you speak.

The Truth About Curse

For those who do not have the understanding of how God works, a thing which must be avoided in life is a curse from God—conventional wisdom. By conventional wisdom, being cursed is a bad thing whether you are guilty or not. I want you to sit back and to see that a curse is actually not a curse. If God created you to fulfill a curse would you do it? It is said that everything came into being from God speaking forth His word. That being said, should you avoid a curse from God, if actually that will bring forth the things He has created you for? Would you receive it faithfully if God spoke not out of anger or not out of you being in the wrong? When you *truly* understand the ways of God, your previous dogma about curse is changed and you see a purpose of God. It was said that he who is hanged on a tree is cursed—does that mean Jesus should not have fulfilled His mission? Does that mean God cursed Jesus? No! However, it was God who sent Him for the cross. Jacob was set apart from his brother Esau after God cursed Esau. If God had not set Jacob apart, we would have been focusing on who is who among Isaac's sons. The same is true for the sons of Abraham, Ishmael and Isaac.

Some have argued that God does not curse. While I agree with those who say such thing (because it is the perception or rationale of an individual that presents a message as a curse or a blessing), I have found that this same people will not permit that principle towards mankind. Because if you say a man cursed when he says exactly what God had said, then that implies God cursed too.

There is a story about two brothers Cain and Abel. Cain killed Abel out of jealousy because God accepted Abel's offering and not his. Look at the act of God here:

"... And now art thou cursed from the earth,...when thou tillest the ground, it shall not henceforth yield unto thee her strength" Gen. 4:11–12. When is cursing acceptable? I am talking to you, O man!

Real Curses from God

"And ye shall eat the flesh of your sons, and the flesh of your daughters shall ye eat."

When bad becomes really bad, it becomes worse and then becomes ugly. We have heard how sometimes a murderer can be as innocent as his/her victim—that is, when God delivers the person into the hand of the so-called murderer to be killed. Let's now direct our attention from worse case to ugly cases, so that you know these things happen by the appointment of God.

In Leviticus, God gave the Israelites statutes and told the Israelites if they didn't do as He commanded He would bring upon them such curse as *"... I will even appoint over you terror, consumption, and the burning ague, that shall consume the eyes, and cause sorrow of heart: and ye shall sow your seed in vain, for your enemies shall eat it. And I will set my face against you, and ye shall be slain before your enemies: they that hate you shall reign over you; and ye shall flee when none pursueth you. ... And your strength shall be spent in vain: for your land shall not yield her increase, neither shall the trees of the land yield their fruits. ...* **And ye shall eat the flesh of your sons, and the flesh of your daughters shall ye eat. ...** *"* Lev. 26:16–35 (Read all in Lev. 26:15–40). When the Israelites faltered in living according to the statutes, God brought upon them a taste of what He promised them—His wrath: *"And it came to pass after this, that Benhadad king of Syria gathered all his host, and went up, and besieged Samaria. And there was a great famine in Samaria: and, behold, they besieged it, until an ass's head was sold for fourscore pieces of silver, and the fourth part of a cab of dove's dung for five pieces of silver. And as the king of Israel was passing by upon the wall, there cried a woman unto him, saying, Help, my lord, O king. And he said, If the LORD do not help thee, whence shall I help thee? out of the barnfloor, or out of the winepress? And the king said unto her, What aileth thee? And she answered, This woman said unto me, Give thy son, that we may eat him to day, and we will eat my son to morrow. So we boiled my son, and did eat him: and I said unto her on the next day, Give thy son, that we may eat him: and she hath hid her son."* 2 Kings 6:24–29. The women ate her son and planned to eat the other woman's son the next day. Now that was an ugly curse. God brought upon the Israelites a taste of what He promised them if they ever faltered in abiding by His statutes. Some of the statutes God expected the Israelites to follow at that time are considered awful or politically not correct in today's living or standard. The statutes included such things as kill the murderer, stone the adulterer, obey the Sabbath, do not turn to idols, do not steal, do not lie, do not deceive one another, do not swear falsely by My name, do not defraud your neighbor or rob him, etc (Read Leviticus in its entirety, especially chapters 17, 18, 19, and 20). Again, where does curse come?

When God wanted to punish David for his bad behavior, God gave David options. What's your choice? The choice is yours. *"... Shall seven years of famine come unto thee in thy land? or wilt thou flee three months before thine enemies, while they pursue thee? or that there be three days' pestilence in thy land? ..."* 2 Sam. 24:13. What will you do when none of the options are favorable to you? David chose the one with the mercy of God attached to it. *"So the LORD sent a pestilence upon Israel from the morning even to the time appointed: and there died of the people from Dan even to Beersheba seventy thousand men."* 2 Sam. 24:15. Did you get that? It was the Lord that sent the pestilence, not the enemy.

"Therefore thus saith the LORD, Behold, I will bring evil upon them, which they shall not be able to escape; and though they shall cry unto me,

I will not hearken unto them." Jer. 11:11. God had brought the curse of the covenant upon Israel. I will say it again: it was God that brought it upon them, not the devil.

It is not that curses do not come from God, the fact is that how can we quickly understand the reasons and purposes behind the curse. For every act of God, there is a good purpose—whether to create, afflict, heal or kill.

Questions to Ponder

When a natural disaster such as earthquake occurs, is that a curse from God?

Is a natural disaster such as a tornado part of God's creation or a curse from God?

Is a bad event a curse or lack of human understanding?

Can any good thing such as a river be formed out of a natural disaster such as an earthquake?

Chapter Five

He Wounds

Fundamentals:

"...I wound, and I heal..." Deu. 32:39.

"The LORD killeth, and maketh alive: he bringeth down to the grave, and bringeth up. The LORD maketh poor, and maketh rich: he bringeth low, and lifteth up. He raiseth up the poor out of the dust, and lifteth up the beggar from the dunghill, to set them among princes, and to make them inherit the throne of glory: for the pillars of the earth are the LORD's, and he hath set the world upon them." 1 Sam. 2:6–8.

"Behold, happy is the man whom God correcteth: therefore despise not thou the chastening of the Almighty: For he maketh sore, and bindeth up: he woundeth, and his hands make whole." Job 5:17–18.

Many have come to know the healing power of God; however, they are ignorant of His afflicting power. But why would God afflict when He heals the wounds of the afflicted? In this chapter, we are going to explore some of the afflictions God had brought upon mankind and the importance of these afflictions as they relate to the growth of mankind in this lifetime and the one to come.

Affliction of the Innocent

Egypt was living large when Abraham was faced with famine in the land the Lord God had asked him to move into and dwell in. So Abraham decided to move to Egypt with his family to survive the famine. Now Abraham had a beautiful wife (Sarah); concerned with the safety of his life coupled with the beauty of his wife—it was possible for him to be killed because of his wife. He decided to lie to the Egyptians and say Sarah was his sister. As a result, Pharaoh took her for himself. What follow afterwards were blessings and afflictions. God blessed Abraham through Pharaoh *"And he entreated Abram well for her sake: and he had sheep, and oxen, and he asses, and menservants, and maidservants, and she asses, and camels."* Gen. 12:16. However, God plagued Pharaoh and his household with great plagues. *"And the LORD plagued Pharaoh and his house with great plagues because of Sarai Abram's wife."* Gen. 12:17.

"And the LORD plagued Pharaoh and his house with great plagues because of Sarai Abram's wife."

Why did God afflict the household of Pharaoh? Does it make sense to bless the liar and afflict the victim of the lie? If God had asked Pharaoh to give Abraham these things without this incident, would Pharaoh have agreed to give anything to Abraham? I tell you what—the answer is a BIG "No." To shake a tree to release its fruits during harvest requires extra force at times. Did Pharaoh deserve a blessing or an affliction?

"And Pharaoh called Abram and said, What is this that thou hast done unto me? why didst thou not tell me that she was thy wife? Why saidst thou, She is my sister? so I might have taken her to me to wife: now therefore behold thy wife, take her, and go thy way." Gen. 12:18–19. Abraham left Pharaoh's house with tons of blessings. Without this shakeup, Pharaoh would not have blessed Abraham the way he blessed him.

A similar incident occurred when Abraham went to Gerar. Abraham yet lied again, saying that Sarah was his sister, this time to Abimelech, the king of Gerar, who took Sarah to have her as his wife. Did God punish Abraham for lying or did He wound Abimelech for taking Sarah? *"But God came to Abimelech in a dream by night, and said* *to him, **Behold, thou art but a dead man**, for the woman which thou hast taken; for she is a man's wife."* Gen. 20:3. In the meantime, God prevented all the women in the household of Abimelech from child bearing because Sarah had been taken. *"For the LORD had fast closed up all the wombs of the house of Abimelech, because of Sarah Abraham's wife."* Gen. 20:18.

I like the petition Abimelech put forth to God: *"But Abimelech had not come near her: and he said, LORD, wilt thou slay also a righteous nation? Said he not unto me, She is my sister? and she, even she herself said, He is my brother: in the integrity of my heart and innocency of my hands have I done this."* Gen. 20:4–5. After it was all finished, Abraham was mightily blessed by God through the hands of Abimelech king of Gerar. *"And Abimelech took sheep, and oxen, and menservants, and womenservants, and gave them unto Abraham, and restored him Sarah his wife. And Abimelech said, Behold, my land is before thee: dwell where it pleaseth thee. And unto Sarah he said, Behold, I have given thy brother a thousand pieces of silver: behold, he is to thee a covering of the eyes, unto all that are with thee, and with all other: thus she was reproved."* Gen. 20:14–16. As the household of Abimelech was still barren, Abraham prayed for Abimelech and his household according to the command of God. *"So Abraham prayed unto God: and God healed Abimelech, and his wife, and his maidservants; and they bare children."* Gen. 20:17.

Now, though it was a loss to those who gave Abraham lots of goods, it was certainly God who was blessing Abraham even though Abraham had lied in the process. Has God caused both Pharaoh and Abimelech to prosper so that out of their prosperity Abraham would be blessed? You bet! Man is known for making big promises before making it big—"I'll share 50/50 with you if I make it"; however, after making it, it is always hard to fulfill that promise.

As it is evident in these events, it was God that made all of these afflictions possible, not Satan, Devil, or the enemies Abimelech or Pharaoh. In today's world, people will blame Satan, Devil, or enemies of various kinds. God was credited with these acts—chiefly the blessings or provisions Abraham received from God through these people in the midst of famine. The part that had always been neglected or ignored without proper crediting is the aspect of God afflicting these people. Let us give credit to whom credit is due. God has been denied credit that is due to Him because of the weakness of human's understanding today. It does not matter whether we think of an event as wicked, painful or not, the credit belongs to God. He afflicts the innocents too.

The Barren Woman

The Bible says we should always give thanks. This is because it is God that makes everything possible. There is no devil or Satan that makes anything possible, only God. In this section, we are going to focus on the childlessness of two women (Rachel and Hannah)

"Am I in God's stead, who hath withheld from thee the fruit of the womb?"

and relate it to their pains and sorrows due to their childless life. ***"And when the LORD saw that Leah was hated, he opened her womb: but Rachel was barren."*** Gen. 29:31. Note that it was God who opened the womb of Leah (Rachel's older sister). *"And when Rachel saw that she bare Jacob no children, Rachel envied her sister; and said unto Jacob, Give me children, or else I die. And Jacob's anger was kindled against Rachel: and he said,* ***Am I in God's stead, who hath withheld from thee the fruit of the womb?"*** Gen. 30:1–2. After much sorrow, Rachel's appointed time came—note that only God can close or open a woman's womb at the appointed time. *"And God remembered Rachel, and God hearkened to her, and opened her womb. And she conceived, and bare a son; and said, God hath taken away my reproach"* Gen. 30:22–23. It is unfortunate that some women who do not want to have children are not barren; and there are countless of women who seek to have children but cannot. However, if they seek the Lord's will for their lives, I am sure they'll find why God has made it to be so. Consider the end result of the story of Jacob's wife Rachel and child bearing. *"And they journeyed from Bethel; and there was but a little way to come to Ephrath: and Rachel travailed, and she had hard labour. And it came to pass, when she was in hard labour, that the midwife said unto her, Fear not; thou shalt have this son also. And it came to pass, as her soul was in departing, (for she died) that she called his name Benoni: but his father called him Benjamin. And Rachel died, and was buried in the way to Ephrath, which is Bethlehem."*

Gen. 35:16–19. Oh sure, Rachel herself desired to reach Bethlehem; but she had compromised one of her desires with her destiny. If God was to tell Rachel that child-bearing would bring an end to her life, would she understand and say to God: Thank you Lord for saving my life? This is one reason why I say God can only talk to you in a way and in the language that YOU can understand. It may be confusing or contradictory or not make sense to someone else; however, it'll make perfect sense to you whom God has spoken to. It is only God that can open or close a woman's womb.

For any barren woman who wants to bear a child, it may be extremely difficult to accept that she is barren, whatever the reasons might be. Now, was Rachel's barrenness the act of God? Nothing happens without the plan of God. At the appointed time, it shall come to pass. Relatively, Hannah was considered barren during the time of Eli the priest. *"But unto Hannah he [her husband Elkanah] gave a worthy portion; for he loved Hannah:* **but the LORD had shut up her womb***."* 1 Sam. 1:5. If Hannah was in any grief because she bore no child, her grief was from God, who shut up her womb. But if Hannah had the understanding and wisdom of God, she would not count it as a pain though she was in the flesh; rather she would thank God for who she was. Nevertheless, in due season and at the appointed time, Hannah gave birth to her first son, he was called Samuel. Her time did not manifest until she had made a vow to God that she would dedicate the son to God for all the days of his life. For all the pains and sorrows these women went through, was that from God or from the devil? I am certain that you know where I stand on this matter.

God's Afflictions

We cannot begin to count God's afflictions on man as we cannot count His blessings on man, because they're too many to be counted—they are uncountable. Here we're going to highlight just a few.

Knowing what God had planned for him, Joseph in the midst of afflictions did not compromise or waver on carrying out the plans God had for him. He kept his covenants with God and did not find any ambiguity in what God had said He would do in his life. This is a story where mankind should say God makes everything for His good pleasure. It may seem odd to you, yet God has a purpose for every

> *For every sequence of events is a manifestation of God's divine plan.*

event. For every sequence of events is a manifestation of God's divine plan. Whether it is within your understanding or not, God is the planner and He has a purpose for it. There is an adage that says everything works together for the goodness of us all.

In an earlier topic we discussed how God planned and hardened Pharaoh's heart so that He (God) could bring to pass His planned signs and wonders so that both the Egyptians and the Israelites would believe that there was God and there was only one God. Let's look at some of the major signs and wonders (afflictions) that God brought upon the Egyptians. For the Israelites these were signs and wonders; however, for the Egyptians these were afflictions. While both stories are true, we have always been taught the stories are true only on the side of the Israelites. Let's now focus on some of the afflictions God brought upon the Egyptians.

There were ten major plagues recorded that came upon Egypt. First, all waters in Egypt were turned into blood. Second, frogs came up and covered the land of Egypt. Third, the dust of the land was turned into lice, and the lice came upon men and animals in the land of Egypt. Fourth, the house of Pharaoh, his servants, and all of Egypt were filled with swarm of flies. Fifth, in one day all the cattle of Egypt died. Sixth, boils came upon both men and animals in all the land of Egypt. Seventh, the Lord rained hails with fire in the land of Egypt, and all living things in the field were killed including men, animals, and all plants in the field. Eighth, the plague of locust came upon Egypt and filled the whole land. Ninth, darkness fell upon Egypt, and Egypt was without daylight for three days. Tenth, the Lord killed the firstborn of every household in Egypt from the firstborn of Pharaoh to the firstborn of every animal. In all these, to the Israelites these were signs and wonders for them to believe and fear God; however, for the Egyptians it was a time of great distress, sorrow, and mourning.

Before the Israelites came to the Promised Land, the land was occupied by several tribes, namely Amorites, Hittites, Perizzites, Canaanites, Hivites, and the Jebusites; however, God had planned that

He would cut off those people and destroy them (and He did) so that the Israelites would take ownership of the land. To these people that were cut off and destroyed, great afflictions came upon them from God. To the Israelites this was a great blessing from God. God said something very significant that is worth mentioning: *"I will not drive them out from before thee in one year; lest the land become desolate, and the beast of the field multiply against thee. By little and little I will drive them out from before thee, until thou be increased, and inherit the land."* Ex. 23:29–30. Does this tell you something? It tells me that God had placed these people in this land to cultivate it while the Israelites were in Egypt and in the wilderness. So while the Israelites were counting their blessings, these tribes were counting their losses and their deaths. It was not because the Israelites were physically stronger than these tribes combined, but it was because God had delivered these inhabitants into the hands of the Israelites to be destroyed.

So while the Israelites were counting their blessings, these tribes were counting their losses and their deaths.

When Miriam and Aaron spoke against Moses, who afflicted Miriam? Miriam became leprous as white as snow in the Lord's anger and she was excluded from the camp for seven days as the Lord commanded. Shouldn't we just get used to the ways of God and stop complaining? When the children of Israel sinned in the sight of God, God delivered them into the hands of the Midianites, who caused them to suffer greatly. God used the Midianites to afflict Israel *"And so it was, when Israel had sown, that the Midianites came up, and the Amalekites, and the children of the east, even they came up against them; And they encamped against them, and destroyed the increase of the earth, till thou come unto Gaza, and left no sustenance for Israel, neither sheep, nor ox, nor ass. For they came up with their cattle and their tents, and they came as grasshoppers for multitude; for both they and their camels were without number: and they entered into the land to destroy it. And Israel was greatly impoverished because of the Midianites; and the children of Israel cried unto the LORD."* Jdg. 6:3–6. Forget about what Israel did!

What is God telling them and us today? In our understanding, there is no justification to starve anyone. Did the Midianites need that food more than the Israelites? I mean, all things being equal, where did this fit in the plan of God? Go figure! This was in fact a type of weapon God used to change or improve the mindset of the Israelites. I'm sure you're asking, the mindset of what? Did Israel learn something out of this? Of course they did.

Remember Gideon, whom God used to lead three hundred men to defeat an army of a size like the sand in the seashore? Gideon served God throughout his life, and throughout his life and leadership, Israel did not depart from the commandments of God. What happened to the household of Gideon after he died? To take the throne of his father, one of Gideon's sons, named Abimelech (son of a maidservant), plotted with his mother's relatives and killed the rest of Gideon's seventy sons, except Jotham, who survived by escaping secretly. *"And he went unto his father's house at Ophrah, and slew his brethren the sons of Jerubbaal, being threescore and ten persons, upon one stone: notwithstanding yet Jotham the youngest son of Jerubbaal [Gideon] was left; for he hid himself."* Jdg. 9:5. Did the faithful servant of God, Gideon, deserve this type of treatment? Was God telling Gideon he didn't need seventy-plus sons to preserve his inheritance? Gideon's household was brutally wounded by God through Abimelech and his conspirators. Do you say that's not true? I ask again, does anything happen without God? Just because you can't comprehend the why, doesn't mean that it was not the power and work of God.

When the Philistines took the Ark of God to their land, was it the devil that afflicted them with emerods? No; it was God who wounded them with that grievous sickness. You think I am making this up? *"But the hand of the LORD was heavy upon them of Ashdod, and he destroyed them, and smote them with emerods, even Ashdod and the coasts thereof."* 1 Sam. 5:6.

During the days of Azariah, king of Judah, son of Amaziah, it was said that he was a God-fearing king; he did, however, overlook the ways of the people of Israel, who were burning incense and sacrificing to strange gods. *"And the LORD smote the king, so that he was a leper unto the day of his death..."* 2Ki. 15:5. Did you get that? It was God that afflicted him with leprosy, not the devil or enemy. Do you hear and still don't understand?

Hear the cry of Ezekiel the priest whose wife was taken away (dead) by God to demonstrate how the Israelites must conduct themselves for the things that is about to come upon them—Ezekiel a sign unto Israel. *"Also the word of the LORD came unto me, saying, Son of man, behold, I take away from thee the desire of thine eyes with a stroke: yet neither shalt thou mourn nor weep, neither shall thy tears run down. Forbear to cry, make no mourning for the dead, bind the tire of thine head upon thee, and put on thy shoes upon thy feet, and cover not thy lips, and eat not the bread of men. So I spake unto the people in the morning: and at even my wife died; and I did in the morning as I was commanded."* Eze. 24:15–18. Could you imagine Ezekiel wife's death was planned by God just to show the Israelites how they had to behave when His afflictions come upon them! *"Thus Ezekiel is unto you a sign: according to all that he hath done shall ye do: and when this cometh, ye shall know that I am the Lord GOD."* Eze. 24:24. Did God take away the life of Ezekiel's wife in order to use him as a sign for the Israelites? Was that what she was created for? You can see how each person is created for his/her unique purpose. This purpose may bring pain and sorrow; however, God said to Ezekiel, do not mourn or cry. This phenomina is applicable to everyone. Suck it up! You can't cry your way out of any difficult situation.

Imagine escaping from being killed and having God say if you escape, wherever you go I will bring death to you. Rather, remain or go back and face any affliction including death instead of escaping. *"Therefore thus saith the LORD of hosts, the God of Israel; Behold, I will set my face against you for evil, and to cut off all Judah. And I will take the remnant of Judah, that have set their faces to go into the land of Egypt to sojourn there, and they shall all be consumed, and fall in the land of Egypt; they shall even be consumed by the sword and by the famine: they shall die, from the least even unto the greatest, by the sword and by the famine: and they shall be an execration, and an astonishment, and a curse, and a reproach. For I will punish them that dwell in the land of Egypt, as I have punished Jerusalem, by the sword, by the famine, and by the pestilence:"* Jer. 44:11–13. And that is not all, God also said, if you escape, whoever abhors you He would also afflict and/or kill because of you—which is what He said to Pharaoh of Egypt. *"Thus saith the LORD; Behold, I will* give Pharaohhophra king of Egypt into the hand of his enemies, and into the hand of them that seek his life; as I gave Zedekiah king of Judah into the hand of Nebuchadrezzar king of Babylon, his enemy, and that sought his life."* Jer. 44:30. Realize though, it is God that is rendering them the afflictions in all of these cases, as He himself had already testified.

Evil Spirit from God

Does God give evil spirits, too? Of course! God afflicted Saul with an evil spirit that troubled and made Saul insane. After God gave the leadership of Israel to Saul, God realized that Saul was not the right person for the leadership of Israel; therefore God began to torment Saul with His evil spirit.

"But the Spirit of the LORD departed from Saul, and an evil spirit from the LORD troubled him."

And it came to pass that during the reign of Saul that Saul became insane because of the evil spirit from God. *"But the Spirit of the LORD departed from Saul, and an evil spirit from the LORD troubled him."* 1 Sam. 16:14. The common and popularly known Spirit of God is the Good Spirit (Spirit of God). The uncommon spirit of God is evident here as God gave a portion of it to Saul—the evil spirit. And could you imagine that in case of Saul the antidote for the evil spirit of God was music? *"And it came to pass, when the evil spirit from God was upon Saul, that David took an harp, and played with his hand: so Saul was refreshed, and was well, and the evil spirit departed from him."* 1 Sam. 16:23.

Maybe Abimelech and the people of Shechem were not aware of the antidote for the evil spirit from God. After Abimelech and the people of Shechem plotted and killed the seventy sons of Gideon and Abimelech had reigned for three years, God said to him and the people of Shechem, I have not finished with you yet! *"Then God sent an evil spirit between Abimelech and the men of Shechem; and the men of Shechem dealt treacherously with Abimelech."* Jdg. 9:23. In the end, both Abimelech and the people of Shechem were destroyed because they were in great confusion from the evil spirit of God that came upon them, as we'll see in the next chapter.

What type of illness if any can legitimately come from God or none whatsoever as we had been thought to believe? During the days of Elisha, the king of Syria became troubled that the king of Israel knew about whatever they discussed behind closed doors. It turned out that whatever they discussed, God revealed it to his servant Elisha in Israel and Elisha in turns revealed it to the king of Israel. When the king of Syria realized the only way to stop this from happening again, he sent his army to go and capture Elisha. *"And when they came down to him, Elisha prayed unto the LORD, and said, Smite this people, I pray thee, with blindness. And he smote them with blindness according to the word of Elisha."* 2Ki. 6:18. So Elisha overcame the chariots of the king of Syria. Can blindness legitimately come from God? Here you have seen it. I can assure you though that the Syrians confessed in those days the truth about who brought the blindness to them—unlike many of today, who say it was the enemy or the devil. The people of Syria at that time said it was the great God of Israel and they were right.

Many of you have argued in the past that God will neither do evil nor will He do evil to His people. During the days of the exodus, the Israelites sinned against God and God said to Moses, step back and let Me consume them; however, Moses appealed to God not to do so and God repented of the evil which He thought of bringing upon the people at that time. *"…nevertheless in the day when I visit I will visit their sin upon them. And the LORD plagued the people…"* Ex. 32:34–35. So, if you're willing to admit it, God indeed does evil (as we'd call it).

Hate or Choice

Many have claimed that God does not hate; however, God with His own words said that He hated Esau and laid his heritage waste. What exactly does that mean? God assigned Esau and Jacob their tasks—however, these assignments were not made in the order of the human understanding. God knowing He was talking to people of lesser understanding in this matter, said this: *"I have loved you, saith the LORD. Yet ye say, Wherein hast thou loved us? Was not Esau Jacob's brother? saith the LORD: yet I loved Jacob, And I hated Esau, and laid his mountains and his heritage waste for the dragons of the wilderness."* Mal. 1:2–3. Certainly, if we as human beings want to bond with the language we currently use, then we have to acclaim that God hates as well when He spoke of Esau. While I agree that we need to improve the way we communicate and better present the message of God, we also have to acknowledge the message in the context of the present language. God has the right to choose whom He desires. However, if God chose one person over another, does that mean God hated the one He did not chose? Of course not! Why are we so naïve? Let's say God has two people, you and someone else. He also has two tasks (X and Y)—these two tasks when completed would bring about one objective He had planned. So that we don't confuse choice and hate—if God chose you to perform task X and you consider that task to be undesirable, does that mean God hated you? On the other hand, if God gave you task Y and the task seem desirable does that mean He hated the other person? Of course not! We need to improve our language. This is where the importance of being spirit-filled comes in. One who is spirit-filled would understand this message better than one who is not spirit-filled. Because our current language has failed to help us to understand God better, we speak a failed language. So next time, when you see the word hate in the Bible, examine it closely in the view of the Kingdom of God rather than in your language or view of this world.

The message is clear; if you think that your situation is painful, sorrowful or painless, look nowhere other than God. Nothing happens under the Sun that God has not ordained. Your situation might be unique, but realize that it is predestined by God. Afflictions will come, and they come from one source: God. How you manage and utilize your afflictions would determine the level of your success.

Questions to Ponder

Can God afflict you, and if so under what circumstances?

Can the evil from God be classified as punishment?

Chapter Six

He Kills

Fundamentals:

"…I kill, and I make alive…" Deu. 32:39.

"The LORD killeth, and maketh alive: he bringeth down to the grave, and bringeth up. The LORD maketh poor, and maketh rich: he bringeth low, and lifteth up. He raiseth up the poor out of the dust, and lifteth up the beggar from the dunghill, to set them among princes, and to make them inherit the throne of glory: for the pillars of the earth are the LORD's, and he hath set the world upon them." 1 Sam. 2:6–8.

"And the LORD said, I will destroy man whom I have created from the face of the earth; both man, and beast, and the creeping thing, and the fowls of the air; for it repenteth me that I have made them." Gen. 6:7.

For many years, mankind had been misguided with the impression that God creates and does not kill. Neglecting the fact that it was God Himself who instituted death in the establishment. Is killing part of the process of life? Does it matter how a person dies? Is there any single way one must die? Does God actually kill or killing is Satan's expertise? In this chapter, we are going to outline how God kills either with His own hands or through other means using several events from the Bible.

Noah's Ark – The Second Beginning

In those days when the wickedness of man became great, God decided that He would destroy every living creature He had made on the face of the earth. Thanks to Noah who found grace in the eyes of God, God decided to spare a few. Thanks to Noah? Was God actually going to destroy every creature including those He spared with Noah?

"For yet seven days, and I will cause it to rain upon the earth forty days and forty nights; and every living substance that I have made will I destroy from off the face of the earth…And it came to pass after seven days, that the waters of the flood were upon the earth…And the waters prevailed exceedingly upon the earth; and all the high hills, that were under the whole heaven, were covered…And all flesh died that moved upon the earth, both of fowl, and of cattle, and of beast, and of every creeping thing that creepeth upon the earth, and every man: All in whose nostrils was the breath of life, of all that was in the dry land, died. And every living substance was destroyed which was upon the face of the ground, both man, and cattle, and the creeping things, and the fowl of the heaven; and they were destroyed from the earth: and Noah only remained alive, and they that were with him in the ark. And the waters prevailed upon the earth an hundred and fifty days." Gen. 7:4, 10, 19, 21–24.

If God said He regretted that He had created man and beast and that it was because of Noah's plea that He preserved man, this meant that God did not know that man would behave this way. This same regret over creating man occurred when man misbehaved in the Garden of Eden. It seems to me then that an unintended consequence was caused by man in God's creation. Was God talking to a people that had only a limited understanding, and that's why He spoke to them this way? God certainly knows the future, as we have previously established. Because of this incident of destruction, God started all over again with creation. Though, this time, it was not with the initial process of creation but with a selected few taken from the said corrupted ones. Based on our understanding today, did that eradication of the living solve the problem God was trying to solve? We can certainly say that it could have been worse today if God had not eradicated the corrupted at that time. Tell me, was God wrong destroying the wicked ones?

Killing in Diverse Measures

There is a story in the Bible commonly told, the story of Sodom and Gomorrah. The Bible says: *"Then the LORD rained upon Sodom and upon Gomorrah brimstone and fire from the LORD out of heaven; And he overthrew those cities, and all the plain, and all the inhabitants of the cities, and that which grew upon the ground."* Gen. 19:24–25. Some stories cannot be fully justified with our mere understanding; however, God knows exactly why they happen. The city of Sodom as we know it was very involved in the practice of homosexual relationships, even to the point where they wanted to forcefully perform that act on the Angels of God, and God said He has seen enough.

God's killings can be measured and justified in some cases and in other cases, you just have to leave it alone but accept the fact that God can kill. God said He would harden Pharaoh's heart so that He could multiply His signs and wonders. When God chooses you for something, whether you think of it as being good or bad, you just have to submit yourself and allow God to do His will—which was exactly what Jesus demonstrated. During the journey with the Israelites to the Promised Land, God wanted to show His power by means of separating and rejoining the sea. Meanwhile, Egypt had already been chosen as the lamb for Israel's sake. God continued to harden the heart of Pharaoh in order that Pharaoh would further pursue the Israelites, and the Egyptians found themselves in the middle of the Red Sea. *"And Moses stretched forth his hand over the sea, and the sea returned to his strength when the morning appeared; and the Egyptians fled against it; and the LORD overthrew the Egyptians in the midst of the sea. And the waters returned, and covered the chariots, and the horsemen, and all the host of Pharaoh that came into the sea after them; there remained not so much as one of them."* Ex. 14:27–28. Thus God divided the Red Sea and killed the Egyptians, and the Israelites feared and believed God. As you can see, Egypt was afflicted for the sake of Israel. The same was true when the Israelites were afflicted for the sake of those that would become believers—which is why Israel is called the elect or chosen one in reference to the believers of today.

The point here is that many of you have argued that God does not kill. Let me give you another insight. God said if anyone afflicts the fatherless or the widow and they cry unto Him, that He will kill that person. *"... I will kill you with the sword; and your wives shall be widows, and your children fatherless."* Ex. 22:24. Therefore, it is not whether God kills, but what is the underlying reason why God kills at any given time. I must note here though that God does not owe you any explanation whatsoever why He kills. Furthermore, God's killing may not make sense to you, and you may even not find any justification for it at times. With the hardness of Pharaoh's heart, God systematically reduced Egypt to a point that was enough (and of course with the fear that got into them) for Israel to live in the Promised Land without Egypt coming to invade Israel, at least in the beginning of Israel's existence.

Sometimes the reason for one being the chosen one is evident, and other times it is not. There is a story about two sons of Aaron, namely Nadab and Abihu, who went and offered sacrifice to God that He had not approved; God immediately set them as an example: *"And there went out fire from the LORD, and devoured them, and they died before the LORD."* Lev. 10:2.

In the midst of a lengthy journey, the Israelites began to complain about almost everything. They complained about hardship *"...and the LORD heard it; and his anger was kindled; and the fire of the LORD burnt among them, and consumed them that were in the uttermost parts of the camp."* Num. 11:1. Thanks to Moses, who prayed to the Lord, the fire was quenched. However, the Israelites didn't learn their lesson from this incident, and they continue to complain. This time they complained about the lack of meat to eat, and God said, I will give you meat to eat and set you as a living example: *"Ye shall not eat one day, nor two days, nor five days, neither ten days, nor twenty days; But even a whole month, until it come out at your nostrils, and it be loathsome unto you..."* Num. 11:19–20. So God supplied quail miraculously, and the Israelites gathered and began to eat, and the anger of God came upon them. Several of them (those who lusted for meat) were killed with the plague.

Killing in the Wild—God's Style

When God decided that those twenty years and older would not come into the Promised Land, it started right away with a plague from

God that killed those that brought the slanderous and evil report about the Promised Land. *"And the men, which Moses sent to search the land, who returned, and made all the congregation to murmur against him, by bringing up a slander upon the land, Even those men that did bring up the evil report upon the land, died by the plague before the LORD."* Num. 14:36–37. These deaths caused the rest of Israel to march forward, now willing to go to the land (they had previously agreed with those who had brought the evil report and had said they'd not go to the land). But Moses commanded them not to move forward, because God would not be in their mix. The Israelites went against Moses' command, and the eradication of the bad ones among them began. *"Then the Amalekites came down, and the Canaanites which dwelt in that hill, and smote them, and discomfited them, even unto Hormah."* Num. 14:45.

Who should be blamed for these killings, the Amalekites and the Canaanites, or God? Since God decreed that this was what must happen, it was a matter of time. It may have presented itself as a war, consequence of disobedience, or some other shape or form, but in the end it was God.

As the journey of the exodus continued, those who had been destined for death in the wilderness (those twenty years and over) got bolder and began to oppose Moses and Aaron. It was not surprising that they revolted, because there had to be justification in order for human beings to understand their eradication. Korah and some members of the council in the community began to oppose Moses and Aaron, claiming that the plan of the exodus was made up by Moses and Aaron so as to lord or rule over the people. But in the midst of them all (Moses, Aaron, Korah and his followers and the rest of the congregation), God proved that the exodus was according to His plan. *"And the earth opened her mouth, and swallowed them up, and their houses, and all the men that appertained unto Korah, and all their goods. They, and all that appertained to them, went down alive into the pit, and the earth closed upon them: and they perished from among the congregation."* Num. 16:32–33. Additionally, fire from the Lord came down and consumed two hundred fifty followers of Korah who were holding

The Acts of God

"And there came out a fire from the LORD, and consumed the two hundred and fifty men that offered incense."

their offerings of incense. *"And there came out a fire from the LORD, and consumed the two hundred and fifty men that offered incense."* Num. 16:35. Then, the Israelites demonstrated against Moses and Aaron, claiming that they had killed the Lord's people. So when God saw the demonstration and accusations of these people saying Moses and Aaron had killed Korah and his followers, God sent a plague among the people and killed fourteen thousand, seven hundred among them before the plague was stopped by Aaron according to Moses' instructions. *"And the LORD spake unto Moses, saying, Get you up from among this congregation, that I may consume them as in a moment. And they fell upon their faces. And Moses said unto Aaron, Take a censer, and put fire therein from off the altar, and put on incense, and go quickly unto the congregation, and make an atonement for them: for there is wrath gone out from the LORD; the plague is begun. And Aaron took as Moses commanded, and ran into the midst of the congregation; and, behold, the plague was begun among the people: and he put on incense, and made an atonement for the people. And he stood between the dead and the living; and the plague was stayed. Now they that died in the plague were fourteen thousand and seven hundred, beside them that died about the matter of Korah."* Num 16:44–49.

The Israelites wept bitterly after God commanded Moses to slay the leaders of those who committed abomination and prostituted themselves with the Moabites regarding Baal-Peor. As they wept, one of their brethren brought in a Midianitish woman into their midst. God said that He had seen enough, and He plagued the people of Israel; twenty-four thousand of them were killed by the plague. Phinehas, Aaron's grandson, killed both the Israelite and the Midianitish woman at once with a spear in the middle of their act, and the plague was stopped. But God commended Phinehas and gave him a covenant of peace. God said to Moses *"Wherefore say, Behold, I give unto him my covenant of peace"* Num.25:12.

Whilst one, few, and thousands died here and there, it was evident that those whom God said would not reach the Promised Land were being eradicated. When the second census of the journey of the exodus was taken, there were six hundred one thousand men, twenty years and over. *"But among these there was not a man of them whom Moses and Aaron the priest numbered, when they numbered the children of Israel in the wilderness of Sinai. For the LORD had said of them, They shall surely die in the wilderness. And there was not left a man of them, save Caleb the son of Jephunneh, and Joshua the son of Nun."* Num. 26:64–65.

Also note that God does not always kill in the most common ways. When the children of Israel spoke against Moses and against God because there was so little bread and water, God sent serpents in their midst. *"And the LORD sent fiery serpents among the people, and they bit the people; and much people of Israel died."* Num. 21:6.

Instrument of Death—Warfare

Though the children of Israel were dying, they were also used by God as instruments of death.

"And the LORD hearkened to the voice of Israel, and delivered up the Canaanites; and they utterly destroyed them and their cities: and he called the name of the place Hormah." Num. 21:3.

"And the LORD said unto Moses, Fear him not: for I have delivered him [Og king of Bashan] into thy hand, and all his people, and his land; and thou shalt do to him as thou didst unto Sihon king of the Amorites, which dwelt at Heshbon. So they smote him, and his sons, and all his people, until there was none left him alive: and they possessed his land." Num. 21:34–35.

Now that the numbered Israelites had all been killed, it was time to focus more on the inhabitants of the Promised Land. Remember the story of Baal-Peor? Because of that, God told Moses to go and avenge the children of Israel for what the Midianites did to the children of Israel in the matter of Baal-Peor. *"And they warred against the Midianites, as the LORD commanded Moses; and they slew all the males. And they slew the kings of Midian, beside the rest of them that were slain; namely, Evi, and Rekem, and Zur, and Hur, and Reba, five kings of Midian: Balaam also the son of Beor they slew with the sword. And the children of Israel took all the women of Midian captives, and their little ones, and took the spoil of all their cattle, and all their flocks, and all their goods."* Num. 31:7–9. When Moses realized that the men that went to the war brought women with them, which was exactly what caused the plague at Baal-Peor, he immediately confronted them. *"And Moses said unto them, Have ye saved all the women alive? Behold, these caused the children of Israel, through the counsel of Balaam, to commit trespass against the LORD in the matter of Peor, and there was a plague among the congregation of the LORD. Now therefore kill every male among the little ones, and kill every woman that hath known man by lying with him. But all the women children, that have not known a man by lying with him, keep alive for yourselves."* Num. 31:15–18. What would have happened to the Israelites if Moses had not ordered them to kill the boys and women that had known men?

In many of the wars that Israel fought, God made advance preparation by stripping their enemy's abilities and hope even before Israel reached the battle ground. In fact, the battle was won even before the war was fought. Before Israel fought in Jericho, Rahab, the harlot who lodged the spies, told the spies that the people of Jericho had been defeated already with fear. *"And she said unto the men, I know that the LORD hath given you the land, and that your terror is fallen upon us, and that all the inhabitants of the land faint because of you. For we have heard how the LORD dried up the water of the Red sea for you, when ye came out of Egypt; and what ye did unto the two kings of the Amorites, that were on the other side Jordan, Sihon and Og, whom ye utterly destroyed. And as soon as we had heard these things, our hearts did melt, neither did there remain any more courage in any man, because of you: for the LORD your God, he is God in heaven above, and in earth beneath."* Jos. 2:9–11. It was after the meltdown of these people's hearts that Israel went in and finished the job and took over Jericho. *"And they utterly destroyed all that was in the city, both man and woman, young and old, and ox, and sheep, and ass, with the edge of the sword."* Jos. 6:21. Realize though that Jericho was destroyed because God has planned it. It was not because Israel lost her mind and went after Jericho.

"And the LORD said unto Joshua, Fear not, neither be thou dismayed: take all the people of war with thee, and arise, go up to Ai: see, I have given into thy hand the king of Ai, and his people, and his city, and his land." Jos. 8:1. In this case of Ai, they were so demoralized that they had no

strength left to flee one way or the other from Israel but instead stood and faced execution. *"And so it was, that all that fell that day, both of men and women, were twelve thousand, even all the men of Ai."* Jos. 8:25. The king of Ai, whom they took alive, was hanged on a tree. But the warfare of God delivering nations into the hands of Israel continued when kings in the surrounding area joined forces to fight Israel; *"And the LORD said unto Joshua, Fear them not: for I have delivered them into thine hand; there shall not a man of them stand before thee. Joshua therefore came unto them suddenly, and went up from Gilgal all night. And the LORD discomfited them before Israel, and slew them with a great slaughter at Gibeon, and chased them along the way that goeth up to Bethhoron, and smote them to Azekah, and unto Makkedah. And it came to pass, as they fled from before Israel, and were in the going down to Bethhoron, that the LORD cast down great stones from heaven upon them unto Azekah, and they died: they were more which died with hailstones than they whom the children of Israel slew with the sword."* Jos. 10:8–11. This sounds like special effects. No, it wasn't; God used an extra arsenal to destroy them—hailstones.

Then God led Israel and they marched on with that combat. This time, they marched over several nations and their kings, starting with Libnah. *"And the LORD delivered it also, and the king thereof, into the hand of Israel; and he smote it with the edge of the sword, and all the souls that were therein; he let none remain in it; but did unto the king thereof as he did unto the king of Jericho. And Joshua passed from Libnah, and all Israel with him, unto Lachish, and encamped against it, and fought against it: And the LORD delivered Lachish into the hand of Israel, which took it on the second day, and smote it with the edge of the sword, and all the souls that were therein, according to all that he had done to Libnah."* Jos. 10:30–32. Then followed Gezer, Eglon, Hebron, Debir, Kadeshbarnea, Gaza, Goshen, and all the way to Gibeon, with Israel warring the entire way. *"So Joshua smote all the country of the hills, and of the south, and of the vale, and of the springs, and all their kings: he left none remaining, but utterly destroyed all that breathed, as the LORD God of Israel commanded."* Jos. 10:40. After this, Joshua and Israel, led by God (or should I say God was hiding behind Israel), went northward to the northern kingdoms. *"And the LORD delivered them into the hand of Israel, who smote them, and chased them unto great Zidon, and unto*

Misrephothmaim, and unto the valley of Mizpeh eastward; and they smote them, until they left them none remaining." Jos. 11:8.

It was not because Israel was stronger than these kingdoms combined; it was because these kingdoms and their kings had been marked for destruction by God. In fact, God hardened their hearts so that they would go to war with Israel and He would have the opportunity to destroy them *"For it was of the LORD to harden their hearts, that they should come against Israel in battle, that he might destroy them utterly, and that they might have no favour, but that he might destroy them, as the LORD commanded Moses."* Jos. 11:20. —God was seeking for an occasion to destroy these people. This is why I said perhaps God was hiding behind the Israelites instead of leading them. Because the people may not have gone to war with Israel if they knew God was the captain of Israel.

In the days of Eli the priest, God went after the sons of Eli, who had been sinning in the sight of God. Though God was after the two sons of Eli, thousands were killed in the process of killing the two sons. *"And the Philistines fought, and Israel was smitten, and they fled every man into his tent: and there was a very great slaughter; for there fell of Israel thirty thousand footmen. And the ark of God was taken; and the two sons of Eli, Hophni and Phinehas, were slain."* 1 Sam. 4:10–11. But it wasn't the will of the so-called devil that said he'd slay them before they were killed by the Philistines. It was God that hardened their hearts that they refused to obey the advice of their father so that He would slay them. *"…Notwithstanding they hearkened not unto the voice of their father, because the LORD would slay them."* 1 Sam. 2:25. In fact, another translation says it was the *Lord's will to put them to death (NIV)*. Though God used the Philistines, it was not the Philistines that killed them but God. The Philistines were only an instrument of death used by God. It was with this understanding that the Lord spoke to Samuel in this manner: *"And the LORD said to Samuel, Behold, I will do a thing in Israel, at which both the ears of every one that heareth it shall tingle."* 1 Sam. 3:11.

During the days of Moses and Joshua, God delivered His and Israel's enemies into the hands of Israel so that they might be destroyed. You know what I found out? God is still in the business of delivering. After the death of Joshua, God said to Judah that He had delivered the land of the Canaanites into Judah's hand and that they should go and get it. *"And Judah went up; and the LORD delivered the Canaanites and the Perizzites into their hand: and they slew of them in Bezek ten thousand men. And they found Adonibezek in Bezek: and they fought against him, and they slew the Canaanites and the Perizzites. But Adonibezek fled; and they pursued after him, and caught him, and cut off his thumbs and his great toes."* Jud. 1:4–6. WOW! Yes, it was payback time. This same Adonibezek confirmed with his own mouth that Israel was not the first to be challenged by God with the dilemma of killing and destroying others. *"And Adonibezek said, Threescore and ten kings, having their thumbs and their great toes cut off, gathered their meat under my table: as I have done, so God hath requited me."* Jud. 1:7. If we knew the prior story of Adonibezek, I have no doubt in my mind that he defeated those seventy kings with the help of God. Did God tell him that if he didn't do this and that, He was going to do unto him what He planned to do unto them? This was exactly what God told the Israelites in their quest for the Promised Land.

Women and Children Too

It is fascinating to hear from all kinds of people when women and children are killed in situations—"many were killed including women and children." As if women and children are exempted from death. There are situations in which God would require you to kill the infants too. Be ready on that day when you'll be required to kill and destroy. What would you say to God, no, Lord I have never killed or destroyed anything in my entire life, or will you say I will do it, or will you say this is the voice of the devil? God instructed Saul through the prophet Samuel to go and utterly destroy the Amalekites, even infants and women. *"Thus saith the LORD of hosts, I remember that which Amalek did to Israel, how he laid wait for him in the way, when he came up from Egypt. Now go and smite Amalek, and utterly destroy all that they have, and spare them not; but slay both man and woman, infant and suckling, ox and sheep, camel and ass."* 1 Sam. 15:2–3.

We usually say the children are innocent! Yeah, right. Children grow up, become adults, and in most cases follow their biological parents rather than those who adopted and bring them up. These same children might even have grown up and become adversaries to Israel. The story of a boy named Hadad comes to mind. Hadad the Edomite escaped to Egypt as a boy during the time when David slew the Edomites; he came back as an adult and became an adversary to Solomon.

And did you know that Saul got into trouble with God for taking home some of the beasts of the land? Oh yes, even the throne of the kingdom of Israel was taken away from him. God wanted to wipe out all the Amalekites from the face of the earth, even to the point that He said *"It repenteth me that I have set up Saul to be king: for he is turned back from following me, and hath not performed my commandments."* 1 Sam. 15:11. You mean God does regret His decisions too? You mean God would ask you to kill too? Very well!

Weapons of Destruction

Throughout history, people die during the time of war; one group defeats or destroys the other; other times, both groups are defeated or destroyed. The reasons are not always because the victorious group was mightier than the losing group. It was because God had marked those losers to be defeated, if not destroyed. Sometimes, the same groups would be all that God needed to eliminate both groups—that is, they killed or destroyed each other, as was evident in the story of Abimelech, son of Gideon, and the men of Shechem (Judges 9). God sent evil spirits among them so that they could destroy and finish each other. *"And Abimelech fought against the city all that day; and he took the city, and slew the people that was therein, and beat down the city, and sowed it with salt."* Jdg. 9:45. Wait—it was not over yet. *"And Abimelech came unto the tower, and fought against it, and went hard unto the door of the tower to burn it with fire. And a certain woman cast a piece of a millstone upon Abimelech's head, and all to brake his skull. Then he called hastily unto the young man his armourbearer, and said unto him, Draw thy sword, and slay me, that men say not of me, A women slew him. And his young man thrust him through, and he died."* Jdg. 9:52–54.

As iron sharpens iron, so also man is the destroyer of man. You can see that the starting and ending point of every event is defined by God—no actor defines his or her role. Thus, God delivered them into the hands of each other. Abimelech and Shechem killed the seventy sons of Gideon, Abimelech killed Shechem, and Shechem killed Abimelech. All to the glory and perfect plan of God!

And there came certain times when the deliverance was turned against Israel, and God delivered them into the hands of their enemies. It was not because God hated them, though it may appear that way to us because we have not understood the ways of God. God did not say Israel would be excluded from discomfort. As far as God was concerned, it was not wrong for Him to deliver them into the hands of their enemies. So God set a stage where Israel was delivered into the hands of her enemies who lived among them. And Israel began to get into that forbidden love—the Israelites went into inter-marriage with their neighbors and served their gods. *"Therefore the anger of the LORD was hot against Israel, and he sold them into the hand of Chushanrishathaim king of Mesopotamia: and the children of Israel served Chushanrishathaim eight years."* Jdg. 3:8. But that was not all that God wanted to do among Israel and her neighbors. In fact, it was time for both Israel and her neighbors to be destroyed (though not altogether). And it came to pass that God delivered Israel to her neighbors, but the Israelites were not completely destroyed, and then Israel's neighbors were delivered to Israel for destruction. This went back and forth throughout the recordings of The Book of Judges.

"And the Spirit of the LORD came upon him [Othniel Judge of Israel], and he judged Israel, and went out to war: and the LORD delivered Chushanrishathaim king of Mesopotamia into his hand; and his hand prevailed against Chushanrishathaim." Jdg. 3:10.

"And the children of Israel did evil again in the sight of the LORD: and the LORD strengthened Eglon the king of Moab against Israel, because they had done evil in the sight of the LORD. And he gathered unto him the children of Ammon and Amalek, and went and smote Israel, and possessed the city of palm trees. So the children of Israel served Eglon the king of Moab eighteen years." Jdg. 3:12–14.

"And Ehud [Judge of Israel] put forth his left hand, and took the dagger from his right thigh, and thrust it into his [Eglon king of Moab] belly: And the haft also went in after the blade; and the fat closed upon the blade, so that he could not draw the dagger out of his belly; and the dirt came out." Jdg. 3:21–22.

"And he [Ehud Judge of Israel] said unto them, Follow after me: for the LORD hath delivered your enemies the Moabites into your hand. And they went down after him, and took the fords of Jordan toward Moab, and

suffered not a man to pass over. And they slew of Moab at that time about ten thousand men, all lusty, and all men of valour; and there escaped not a man." Jdg. 3:28–29.

So, though Israel was the chosen one, they were not exempted from facing the due process of God.

God said to Gideon that the number of people he had were too many for Him (God) to clearly take all the credit. *"And the LORD said unto Gideon, The people that are with thee are too many for me to give the Midianites into their hands, lest Israel vaunt themselves against me, saying, Mine own hand hath saved me."* Jdg. 7:2. Now the number of men God was talking about was thirty-two thousand. After the smoke was cleared, with just three hundred men, Israel wiped out an army described to be like the sand on the seashore.

We have established in many ways that one can only be killed if God delivers that person into the hand of the instrument of death—that instrument can be someone or it can be other forms that God uses both commonly and uncommonly. In the story of David and Goliath, David succeeded in killing Goliath the Philistine only because God delivered him into the hand of David the Israelite. *"This day will the LORD deliver thee into mine hand…"* 1 Sam. 17:46. As was evident, Goliath wasn't a small man; rather, it was David who was the youth. Yet, because God had delivered Goliath into the hands of David, there was nothing Goliath could do with his mighty strength and macho status but to die with the least weapon. *"And David put his hand in his bag, and took thence a stone, and slang it, and smote the Philistine in his forehead, that the stone sunk into his forehead; and he fell upon his face to the earth."* 1 Sam. 17:49.

Before God killed Ahab, king of Israel (but not Judah), and his wife Jezebel, God revealed it through the prophet Elijah. With the persuasion of his wife, Ahab went and killed a man named Naboth and took his land—so the Lord spoke: *"…Hast thou killed, and also taken possession? And thou shalt speak unto him, saying, Thus saith the LORD, In the place where dogs licked the blood of Naboth shall dogs lick thy blood, even thine."* 1Ki. 21:19. But for Jezebel, his wife, a harsher punishment was pronounced on her because she was the spearhead of Ahab's evil: *"And of Jezebel also spake the LORD, saying, The dogs shall eat Jezebel by the wall of Jezreel. Him that dieth of Ahab in the city the dogs shall eat; and him that dieth in the field shall the fowls of the air eat."* 1Ki. 21:23–24.

When Ahab died in the battle of Ramoth Gilead, his dead body was brought to Samaria and the dogs licked his blood, which fulfilled the word of the Lord. And beginning with Ahab's son, Jehoram, Jehu king of Israel, killed the household of Ahab. *"And Jehu drew a bow with his full strength, and smote Jehoram between his arms, and the arrow went out at his heart, and he sunk down in his chariot. Then said Jehu to Bidkar his captain, Take up, and cast him in the portion of the field of Naboth the Jezreelite: for remember how that, when I and thou rode together after Ahab his father, the LORD laid this burden upon him; Surely I have seen yesterday the blood of Naboth, and the blood of his sons, saith the LORD; and I will requite thee in this plat, saith the LORD. Now therefore take and cast him into the plat of ground, according to the word of the LORD."* 2Ki. 9:24–26.

Now Ahab had seventy sons in Samaria; and it came to pass that Jehu, king of Israel, sent for the people of Samaria to send to him the heads of the sons of Ahab in a basket. *"And it came to pass, when the letter came to them, that they took the king's sons, and slew seventy persons, and put their heads in baskets, and sent him them to Jezreel."* 2Ki. 10:7. However, that wasn't all in the household of Ahab that God said must be destroyed. *"Know now that there shall fall unto the earth nothing of the word of the LORD, which the LORD spake concerning the house of Ahab: for the LORD hath done that which he spake by his servant Elijah. So Jehu slew all that remained of the house of Ahab in Jezreel, and all his great men, and his kinsfolks, and his priests, until he left him none remaining."* 2Ki. 10:10–11.

"And when he came to Samaria, he slew all that remained unto Ahab in Samaria, till he had destroyed him, according to the saying of the LORD, which he spake to Elijah." 2Ki. 10:17.

So what happened to Jezebel? I'm glad you asked! *"And when Jehu was come to Jezreel, Jezebel heard of it; and she painted her face, and tired her head, and looked out at a window. And as Jehu entered in at the gate, she said, Had Zimri peace, who slew his master? And he lifted up his face to the window, and said, Who is on my side? who? And there looked out to him two or three eunuchs. And he said, Throw her down. So they threw her down: and some of her blood was sprinkled on the wall, and on the horses: and he trode her under foot. And when he was come in, he did eat and drink, and said, Go, see now this cursed woman, and bury her: for she is a king's daughter. And they went to bury her: but they found no more of her than the skull, and the feet, and the palms of her hands. Wherefore they came again, and told him. And he said, This is the word of the LORD, which he spake by his servant Elijah the Tishbite, saying, In the portion of Jezreel shall dogs eat the flesh of Jezebel: And the carcase of Jezebel shall be as dung upon the face of the field in the portion of Jezreel; so that they shall not say, This is Jezebel."* 2Ki. 9:30–37. So the word of the Lord came to pass as it was spoken by the prophet. You can see that different people die different ways!

God with His Own Hands

For those of you who have not been convinced that God kills, let me shed a light into your understanding. God killed a man named Nabal. Who killed him? God did. *"And it came to pass about ten days after, that the LORD smote Nabal, that he died."* 1 Sam. 25:38. Keep in mind, as God estabished the beginning of life, so also He establihed the end of life according to His purpose and plan. During the time when the ark of God was at the house of Abinadab, it came to be that the ark was to be moved to Jerusalem. Two sons of Abinadab, Uzzah and Ahio, were required to guide the cart as it went on its way to Jerusalem. *"And when they came to Nachon's threshingfloor, Uzzah put forth his hand to the ark of God, and took hold of it; for the oxen shook it. And the anger of the LORD was kindled against Uzzah; and God smote him there for his error; and there he died by the ark of God."* 2 Sam. 6:6–7. What was God telling us? I thought Uzzah was trying to help! Was this an error or a helping hand? Was God saying that Uzzah should have left the ark to fall? But because Uzzah held the ark from falling, God killed him. Can you find the justification of God's action? Similar justification was used in the matter of "Water from the Rock" that prevented Moses and Aaron from reaching the Promised Land. Moses was asked by God to speak to the rock so it would pour out water for the people to drink—God wanted to use the event to show the Israelites He is a God of holiness and would not violate His word. He wanted them to trust Him even when it seems impossible. He wanted to show them if they remained in Him, out of their mouth is power to overcome anything. God wanted Moses to honor Him in the presence of them all that He is their provider in times of their need. However, Moses struck the rock twice with his staff and the miracle which God intended to fulfill was obscured by Moses' actions. No one knew what God intended to do as the ark was falling; howbeit, the actions of Uzzah prevented that possible phenomenon from happening.

In regards to what brought about the first king of Israel, Saul, God said that He appointed him and also brought to an end his reign. *"I gave thee a king in mine anger, and took him away in my wrath."* Hos. 13:11. Though God Himself testifies that He does all these things, we as humans are not willing to admit that God does such things. If there is no time for birth and no time for death where would the earth be? Even the process of agriculture is designed in this way.

"I gave thee a king in mine anger, and took him away in my wrath."

God does not only afflict or kill kings and the ordinary; men of God are not exempted either. *"And when he was gone, a lion met him by the way, and slew him: and his carcase was cast in the way, and the ass stood by it, the lion also stood by the carcase."* 1Ki. 13:24." This was a man of God whom God told he must neither eat nor drink in the place where He would send him. Though he did not eat or drink and left the place, another man who claimed to be a man of God deceived him into going back to the place where he had earlier left. They returned and ate together. So when God is killing, there is no exceptions and favoritism. And did you notice that the lion did not kill or eat the ass? Was it the desire of the lion to slay the man of God, or did God deliver him into the lion's hand?

Everyone will die one day or another; whether you're rich or poor, slave or free, social upper class or social lower class; whether you are killed, murdered, executed, or die from illness or age, death will come some day. Only a few are taken up without seeing death or a grave being assigned to their names. It was God that instituted death and death come in various forms—at the appointed time of God.

Questions to Ponder

Does God kill, and if yes, why?

Does God kill, and if no, why?

What are some of the instruments that God uses to kill?

Are there justifications to kill women and children at times?

Chapter Seven

He Deserves the Credit and the Blame

Fundamentals:

"And if a man lie not in wait, but God deliver him into his hand; then I will appoint thee a place whither he shall flee." Ex. 21:13.

"And the LORD God said unto the serpent, Because thou hast done this, thou art cursed above all cattle, and above every beast of the field; upon thy belly shalt thou go, and dust shalt thou eat all the days of thy life: And I will put enmity between thee and the woman, and between thy seed and her seed; it shall bruise thy head, and thou shalt bruise his heel. Unto the woman he said, I will greatly multiply thy sorrow and thy conception; in sorrow thou shalt bring forth children; and thy desire shall be to thy husband, and he shall rule over thee. And unto Adam he said, Because thou hast hearkened unto the voice of thy wife, and hast eaten of the tree, of which I commanded thee, saying, Thou shalt not eat of it: cursed is the ground for thy sake; in sorrow shalt thou eat of it all the days of thy life; Thorns also and thistles shall it bring forth to thee; and thou shalt eat the herb of the field; In the sweat of thy face shalt thou eat bread, till thou return unto the ground; for out of it wast thou taken: for dust thou art, and unto dust shalt thou return." Gen. 3:14–19.

> *"I also will not henceforth drive out any from before them of the nations which Joshua left when he died: That through them I may prove Israel, whether they will keep the way of the LORD to walk therein, as their fathers did keep it, or not. Therefore the LORD left those nations, without driving them out hastily; neither delivered he them into the hand of Joshua." Jdg. 2:21–23.*

> *"And it repented the LORD that he had made man on the earth, and it grieved him at his heart." Gen. 6:6.*

We have concluded that God knows everything, including the future. Why then is God blaming and repenting that He had made man, beasts, and the fowls of the air after the wickedness of man had become great? Truly one can argue that because he or she knows the future does not exclude him or her from being grieved when something bad happens. I supposed that God should know and expect these things to happen. It has to be human beings that are blaming one another. I don't believe that God would blame someone else while He has control over everything. Is this behavior of human beings not included in the initial plan of God? Does anything happen that God did not plan or know about? If God did not plan it, why then did He allow it to happen? Are we saying that things can happen without God? Let's dig deeper. Let's establish the facts and reasons why we must give God both the credit and the blame—giving power and authority of any kind to Satan undermines the authority of God.

Blame Me

Consider Pharaoh of Egypt during the days of Moses. Though God Himself hardened his heart, Pharaoh was blamed for not letting the people of Israel go. Who should be blamed for the wickedness of Pharaoh? After all, God said He hardened Pharaoh's heart, and it is God Himself who made man and put all man's thoughts into man. Many of you have agreed that everything happens according to God's plan; why then are we blaming someone else when disaster strikes? In our human understanding, many of us have been brought up not

"And if a man lie not in wait, but God deliver him into his hand; then I will appoint thee a place whither he shall flee."

to blame God for anything. However, God indicated that we should blame Him in certain types of events. *"And if a man lie not in wait, but God deliver him into his hand; then I will appoint thee a place whither he shall flee."* Ex. 21:13. The question then is, will God make or lead you to kill someone? Here God is saying He may cause you to kill someone. What will happen to the one who does the killing if his neighbors did not know that it was God who delivered the dead man into the hand of the killer? That killer's life is also in danger of death.

A typical example is taken from the Book of Numbers, where the Israelites fell into the hands of the Amalekites and the Canaanites. This happened after God said to the Israelites that those people twenty years and over would not enter the Promised Land. *"Then the Amalekites came down, and the Canaanites which dwelt in that hill, and smote them, and discomfited them, even unto Hormah."* Num. 14:45. Who should be blamed for these killings: the Amalekites and the Canaanites or God? They might just as easily have died in a war or other ways; this was the plan of God.

Another example is related to fulfilling the Law. If a man is stoned to death by his fellows because he labored on the Sabbath, who is to be blamed? Obviously they're in obedience fulfilling the Law. *"And while the children of Israel were in the wilderness, they found a man that gathered sticks upon the sabbath day. And they that found him gathering sticks brought him unto Moses and Aaron, and unto all the congregation. And they put him in ward, because it was not declared what should be done to him. And the LORD said unto Moses, The man shall be surely put to death: all the congregation shall stone him with stones without the camp. And all the congregation brought him without the camp, and stoned him with stones, and he died; as the LORD commanded Moses."* Num. 15:32–36. When a state death penalty executioner executes someone according to the law of the land, is it the executioner who is blamed or the state? Obviously it is the state. And so it is in the things of God.

When the children of Israel blamed Moses and Aaron for killing the people of God in the matter of Korah (Numbers 16), God plagued them and about fourteen thousand seven hundred of the people were killed. Very often, because of our lack of understanding, we blame this person and that person in all kinds of matters. Though their disobedience is also being measured in this case, God has said that they should not give His credit to someone else by means of blaming someone. Anytime God does not speak up, man takes the blame. Note, however, man is blamed because of our lack of understanding.

In today's world, due to the freedom we preach to one another, we allow all kinds of behavior in our midst. In ancient days, God did not allow the Israelites to keep any 'bad apple' among them. A story was recorded in the journey of the exodus where some of the Israelites started hanging out with the Moabites and having sexual relationships with them. They were eating foods that were sacrificed to their gods and bowing down to their gods. God got angry, and He said to Moses that he should get rid of these bad people in their midst before things get out of control and before He killed more than necessary. *"And the LORD said unto Moses, Take all the heads of the people, and hang them up before the LORD against the sun, that the fierce anger of the LORD may be turned away from Israel. And Moses said unto the judges of Israel, Slay ye every one his men that were joined unto Baalpeor."* Num. 25:4–5. So the Israelites killed them as Moses directed them through the commandment of God. God will not always open the earth or bring down fire from heaven to extinct or kill those that are due for death. Man is an instrument that God uses. So then, who's taking the blame?

Fulfilling Your Destiny

If I am fulfilling my God-given destiny, why am I being blamed? How can one who does not have control of his/her mind be blamed for anything resulting from the mind? How can one who does not have control of his/her destiny be blamed for the outcome of what they have done? How can one who does not have control over his/her direction be blamed for the result of the direction he/she has taken? Who should take the blame if we're only fulfilling our destiny, the law, and the commandments? Who should take the blame if we're only actors in the plan

Do not think that those things you do that are successful are of your destiny and from God and those that are unsuccessful are not your destiny and not from God.

of God? It is not that we should blame God; rather, it is that we should strive to better understand Him. If you fully understand the things of God, those things that you find to be bad are really not bad as you think. Do not think that those things you do that are successful are of your destiny and from God and those that are unsuccessful are not your destiny and not from God. Whether successful or unsuccessful, they're both part of your destiny and perfectly planned by God. All you need to do is change the way you think about things or situations. You cannot choose anything other than what you were created for. You mean I don't have a choice? Not with God. As you walk with God, you begin to understand things in the Kingdom level and your choices will be aligned with the plan and destiny God has for you. We are created to function dynamically; however, each step of the way is known by God even before we take the step.

Let's look further into some of the laws and commandments God gave to mankind, and what God said we should do in each case so that you'll know what is expected of you.

Regarding your brother who attempts to lead you to a god you do not know: *"But thou shalt surely kill him; thine hand shall be first upon him to put him to death, and afterwards the hand of all the people. And thou shalt stone him with stones, that he die; because he hath sought to thrust thee away from the LORD thy God…"* Deu. 13:9–10.

Regarding the false prophet: *"But the prophet, which shall presume to speak a word in my name, which I have not commanded him to speak, or that shall speak in the name of other gods, even that prophet shall die."* Deu. 18:20.

Regarding a stubborn and rebellious son who refused to take corrections from his parents and from the elders of the city: *"And all the men of his city shall stone him with stones, that he die: so shalt thou put evil away from among you…"* Deu. 21:21.

The Acts of God

In order for God's plan to be complete, you have to fulfill your God-given destiny; because your destiny is one part of God's overall plan. God used the Canaanites to teach Israel lesson, and He used Gideon, an Israelite, to teach the Canaanites lesson—all to His glory. Why would God ask Gideon to go and destroy the Canaanites? What justification did Gideon assert when he went and avenged the children of Israel that were slain when God delivered them to the king of Canaan (Judges 4)? Was it the fault of the Canaanites that God sold Israel to them? Meanwhile, God was with Gideon when he went and avenged the children of Israel. What is God telling us? After all, He delivered the Israelites into the hands of the Canaanites. Gideon slew the Canaanites, and when Gideon returned from his pursuit of Zebah and Zalmunna, the kings of the Midian, he went and confronted the people of Succoth for taunting him while he was in pursuit of Zebah and Zalmunna— the elders he put to shame and the men he slew. *"Then said he unto Zebah and Zalmunna, What manner of men were they whom ye slew at Tabor? And they answered, As thou art, so were they; each one resembled the children of a king. And he said, They were my brethren, even the sons of my mother: as the LORD liveth, if ye had saved them alive, I would not slay you. And he said unto Jether his firstborn, Up, and slay them. But the youth drew not his sword: for he feared, because he was yet a youth. Then Zebah and Zalmunna said, Rise thou, and fall upon us: for as the man is, so is his strength. And Gideon arose, and slew Zebah and Zalmunna, and took away the ornaments that were on their camels' necks."* Jdg. 8:18–21. So Gideon destroyed the Canaanites whom God used to teach Israel a lesson. It was God's plan to destroy Canaan through Gideon, and it was His plan to deliver Israel to the Canaanites. This plan of Gideon destroying the Canaanites was part of Gideon's destiny and God's plan for his life. There is a reason the Bible says in all things give thanks. Those who have the understanding of how God does things are always thankful whether in good or bad situations. My blaming God here is not because I don't understand, but to paint you a picture of how God's plan works so that you may see and appreciate everything and not just some things. I am blaming God in appreciation—I am giving Him the credit of what He has done.

Again, if I fulfill my God-given destiny, why should I be blamed? No—God is taking the blame. While God is taking the blame, you should change the way you look at things, so that you'll no longer be blaming God. Rather, you'll give Him credit that He deserves. He deserves your praise and appreciation.

Consequence of Disobedience

During the massive wars that Israel undertook, God gave them specific instructions regarding sparing the inhabitants in their conquest for the Promised Land—the instruction was to put everyone to the sword. However, like every task, man would be exhausted after killing so much, after that, man will cherry-pick among the remnants. When Israel got to that limit, they spared some. *"There was none of the Anakims left in the land of the children of Israel: **only in Gaza, in Gath, and in Ashdod, there remained.**"* Jos. 11:22. These people from Gaza, Gath, and Ashdod are some of the remnants that are pricking Israel today. God said He would do to Israel what He planned to do to the inhabitants of the land that they were about to possess, if they spared anyone. God also said that He would not completely remove the inhabitants of the land at once because He didn't want the land to be desolate. Did you see the coincident? God said that He would not drive them out at once; when Israel got to that stage in the invasion, they spared some unintentionally. See how the plan came together? Remember that there is no one who can claim permanent residency on this earth. This planet is for a sojourn purpose. People come and go; considering it a permanent place is a misunderstanding in one's part. The question here is this, will these leftovers be the people that will destroy Israel?

Will God use Gaza, Ashdod, and Gath to eliminate Israel? *"Therefore it shall come to pass, that as all good things are come upon you, which the LORD your God promised you; so shall the LORD bring upon you all evil things, until he have destroyed you from off this good land which the LORD your God hath given you. When ye have transgressed the covenant of the LORD your God, which he commanded you..."* Jos. 23:15–16. This I believe is a hint that Israel will be destroyed; because Israel has already transgressed in the commandments of God. Yet they may not be completely destroyed; who will raise her hand to touch the Lord's chosen nation except the Lord Himself?

Did Joshua make a mistake when he spared some inhabitants of the land they went to possess? Did I not tell you that God has plans for everything? Remember when God said to Israel that He would not drive out the inhabitants at once? It turns out that God used these same people to prove Israel's loyalty to Him and to make sure that Israel continues to follow His ways. *"I also will not henceforth drive out any from before them of the nations which Joshua left when he died: That through them I may prove Israel, whether they will keep the way of the LORD to walk therein, as their fathers did keep it, or not. Therefore the LORD left those nations, without driving them out hastily; neither delivered he them into the hand of Joshua."* Jdg. 2:21–23. Now you can see that these people seem to be of purpose. So, should we blame Joshua and the Israelites for keeping them because we lack the understanding, or should we blame God? We have in fact blamed Israel in the past; however, as it is, neither Israel nor God is to be blamed. Rather, we need to improve our understanding of how God works and does things.

We tend to blame ourselves when things go wrong. It is about time mankind begins to understand God better and stop blaming one another. If God needs to go against Israel for His plans to succeed, that is exactly what He will do. *"And the anger of the LORD was hot against Israel, and he delivered them into the hands of spoilers that spoiled them, and he sold them into the hands of their enemies round about, so that they could not any longer stand before their enemies. Whithersoever they went out, the hand of the LORD was against them for evil, as the LORD had said, and as the LORD had sworn unto them: and they were greatly distressed."* Jdg. 2:14–15. The Bible says that God is not a respecter of persons. God will use anyone to fulfill His plans. It is therefore necessary that we stop blaming one another. God established that Israel was not excluded from His wrath, and that He would do to Israel exactly what He has planned to do to the inhabitants they replaced.

Before Babylon took Israel captive and exiled them for seventy years, God spoke through His prophets, including Jeremiah, saying what He has planned to do. *"Behold, I will send and take all the families of the north, saith the LORD, and Nebuchadrezzar the king of Babylon, my servant, and will bring them against this land, and against the inhabitants thereof, and against all these nations round about, and will utterly destroy them, and make them an astonishment, and an hissing, and perpetual desolations. Moreover I will take from them the voice of mirth, and the voice of gladness, the voice of the bridegroom, and the voice of the bride, the sound of the millstones, and the light of the candle. And this whole land shall be a desolation, and an astonishment; and these nations shall serve the king of Babylon seventy years."* Jer. 25:9–11.

And it came to pass that the king of Babylon took Israel captive. *"In the ninth year of Zedekiah king of Judah, in the tenth month, came Nebuchadrezzar king of Babylon and all his army against Jerusalem, and they besieged it. And in the eleventh year of Zedekiah, in the fourth month, the ninth day of the month, the city was broken up."* Jer. 39:1–2. But while Babylon took Israel captive, God also indicated that after Babylon had completed her assignment (that is, captivity and exile of Israel) He would bring punishment to Babylon herself. *"And it shall come to pass, when seventy years are accomplished, that I will punish the king of Babylon, and that nation, saith the LORD, for their iniquity, and the land of the Chaldeans, and will make it perpetual desolations."* Jer. 25:12. God said the reason why He would bring Babylon down is because her intentions were wrong though she did what God asked her to do. *"Because ye were glad, because ye rejoiced, O ye destroyers of mine heritage, because ye are grown fat as the heifer at grass, and bellow as bulls;"* Jer. 50:11. Babylon had completed her God-given assignment; it was time for Babylon to cease existing—A typical description of every creation: birth, fulfillment (work), and then finally to die. No exceptions.

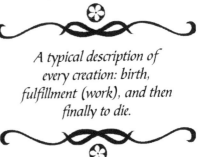

A typical description of every creation: birth, fulfillment (work), and then finally to die.

What if the northern kingdoms disobeyed God and had not overthrown the cities of Judah? What would be the consequence of their disobedience or refusal? Should their refusal be considered disobedient? Notice that Nebuchadrezzar, king of Babylon, was a servant to the God of Israel, the one through whom God put the Israelites into captivity and sent them into exile for seventy years. Note also that the king was punished by God after the seventy years was completed (that is, after he had fulfilled his mission). So in all these, on whom shall the blame lie? You can see that it is God who makes all things possible.

What disobedience are we talking about? That a man refused to kill his fellow man even though God asked him to do it? It does not matter what assignment is in your destiny; you have the responsibility to fulfill it. Disobedience is not only when you refuse to do what you were asked to do; if you grumble or rejoice where you're not supposed to, or make your intentions contrary to God's plan, that is disobedience as well. Earlier we talked about death and how it came about and how God prevented man from eating from the 'tree of life'; if man finds the 'tree of life' today and eats from it, in order to live forever, will that be disobedience? YES! Furthermore, if God has established that at certain point in the human race man will be introduced to that 'tree of life' so that man will live forever, it shall come to pass. And the credit is unto God and not man and his scientific advancements.

Give God the Credit

In any event, if we give God the credit, who should take the blame? God said to Gideon it appeared that Israel might claim the credit for this war. Therefore he should reduce his army so that Israel would not think that they deserved any credit. Let me tell you this, credit and blame are used interchangeably; one is used on a positive tone while the other on a negative tone. *"And the LORD said unto Gideon, The people that are with thee are too many for me to give the Midianites into their hands, lest Israel vaunt themselves against me, saying, Mine own hand hath saved me."* Jdg. 7:2. So Israel became victorious with just three hundred men instead of thirty-two thousand men against an army described to be like the sand on the seashore. It is the one who takes the credit to whom the blame is also due; because while Israel was thanking God for their victory, the Midianites were blaming God—not Gideon—for their defeat. Shouldn't God also have received the blame by the Midianites?

Who took the blame for the killing madness when God decided that He would take away the kingdom from Solomon and would temporarily place it into the hands of some others? First let us examine the prophecy against Jeroboam, the officer of Solomon who rebelled against him, one of the adversaries God sent to Solomon: *"Therefore, behold, I will bring evil upon the house of Jeroboam, and will cut off from Jeroboam him that pisseth against the wall, and him that is shut up and left in Israel, and will take away the remnant of the house of Jeroboam, as a man taketh away dung, till it be all gone. Him that dieth of Jeroboam in the city shall the dogs eat; and him that dieth in the field shall the fowls of the air eat: for the LORD hath spoken it. Arise thou therefore, get thee to thine own house: and when thy feet enter into the city, the child shall die. And all Israel shall mourn for him, and bury him: for he only of Jeroboam shall come to the grave, because in him there is found some good thing toward the LORD God of Israel in the house of Jeroboam. Moreover the LORD shall raise him up a king over Israel, who shall cut off the house of Jeroboam that day: but what? even now. For the LORD shall smite Israel, as a reed is shaken in the water, and he shall root up Israel out of this good land, which he gave to their fathers, and shall scatter them beyond the river, because they have made their groves, provoking the LORD to anger."* 1Ki. 14:10–15. What other way can one take away a throne from a family besides killing all the males in that family?

After the death of Jeroboam, his son Nadab reigned in Israel. To fulfill the prophecy, God raised up Baasha, and he killed Nadab. *"Even in the third year of Asa king of Judah did Baasha slay him, and reigned in his stead. And it came to pass, when he reigned, that he smote all the house of Jeroboam; he left not to Jeroboam any that breathed, until he had destroyed him, according unto the saying of the LORD, which he spake by his servant Ahijah the Shilonite."* 1Ki. 15:28–29.

Wow! To whom should Baasha have given credit for his success? Baasha would definitely have given the credit to God, who raised and predestined him to destroy the household of Jeroboam. And what happened to Baasha? He reigned twenty-four years in Israel and was delivered by God for destruction because he had fulfilled his mission. This may be revealing to some of you, because in the past, you have focused on Baasha's straying from God as the reason for his destruction. The question you should ask yourself is whether God intended the descendants of Baasha to bring to being the Holy One of Israel? And the answer you would find is a no. This was the prophecy that led to his death *"Behold, I will take away the posterity of Baasha, and the posterity of his house; and will make thy house like the house of Jeroboam the son of Nebat. Him that dieth of Baasha in the city shall the dogs eat; and him that dieth of his in the fields shall the fowls of the air eat."* 1Ki. 16:3–4. It was Zimri, his servant, who conspired and killed him while he was drunk and took the kingship. *"And it came to pass, when he began to reign, as soon as he sat on his throne, that he slew all the house of Baasha: he left him not one that pisseth against a wall, neither of his kinsfolks, nor of his friends. Thus did Zimri destroy all the house of Baasha, according to the word of the LORD, which he spake against Baasha by Jehu the prophet."* 1Ki. 16:11–12. As for Zimri, he committed suicide after Israel rebelled against him for killing the king.

Now Ahab, son of Omri, became king of Israel after his father. And it came to pass that God asked Ahab to utterly destroy Ben-Hadad king of Aram. However, Ahab ended up having a treaty with Ben-Hadad. And the man of God delivered the word of the Lord to Ahab. *"And he said unto him, Thus saith the LORD, Because thou hast let go out of thy hand a man whom I appointed to utter destruction, therefore thy life shall go for his life, and thy people for his people."* 1Ki. 20:42. But Ahab humbled himself before God, and God said He would not do unto him the evil He had planned against his household during his life time; however, He would do it during the reign of Ahab's son. *"And the word of the LORD came to Elijah the Tishbite, saying, Seest thou how Ahab humbleth himself before me? because he humbleth himself before me, I will not bring the evil in his days: but in his son's days will I bring the evil upon his house."* 1Ki. 21:28–29. Now, whoever killed Ahab's son and the rest of Ahab's household, should anyone else have been blamed? Wasn't it a premeditated plan from God? God raised Jehu, who carried out the plan as it was revealed in our prior chapter. Who should have been blamed for the death of Ahab after God had proclaimed death for him? And it came to pass that king Ahab went to war and was hit by a bow. *"So the king died, and was brought to Samaria; and they buried the king in Samaria. And one washed the chariot in the pool of Samaria; and the dogs licked up his blood; and they washed his armour; according unto the word of the LORD which he spake."* 1Ki. 22:37–38.

Just so you know, God was not planning on using the descendants of these people to bring about the everlasting One. In order for the appointed time to come in its due season, something has to take place while the season awaits its time. This process is likened unto a farmer who plants his crops during the planting seasons; he continues to cultivate and nurse the soil and crops so that at the due season of harvest, he may harvest to the fullest. What God did was exactly that; He provided

God decides the outcome of every event, and He takes credit for all outcomes.

sustenance for the people until the appointed time. The path to your destiny and the stages of life progress must not be discredited or ignored.

God is not blaming anyone for the outcome of any event; but rather, we have not reached that level of knowledge where we view all things good. You may at times think that the outcome of an event was a result of what you did contrary to what God has planned. Let me warn you that is a wrong perception. God decides the outcome of every event, and He takes credit for all outcomes.

In the beginning (during the establishment) when God made the declaration about the rules of engagement here on earth to man (Genesis 3), it was due to the test result God received about man, His latest creation. Based on the test result, God knew it was time to apply the rules necessary for man. It was not because of man's misstep, but rather the appointed time for God to define the fundamentals or the rules of engagement here on earth to man.

Consider the very first creations: the earth was formless; darkness was created before light, and light was created out of darkness. It was not because darkness did something wrong that God decided to create light. God created the food necessary for man before He created man. Man was created before woman was created to help the man. So also the rules for man were created after man. Why did God create them in this order? I don't know. What I do know is that His sequences of choices are precise and well-suited. The creation was one after another. The only blame man carries with him at all times is the fact that he thinks of himself all the time. God created man in His own likeness. So man has a mind like God. Because of this, man's thinking process is geared towards more to self than anything else. This truth is revealed when God spoke about why He would destroy the Babylonians in regards to their captivity and exile of Israel. Though they did what He commissioned them to do and fulfilled His plan, God said their intentions were wrong. *"Because ye were glad, because ye rejoiced, O ye destroyers of mine heritage, because ye are grown fat as the heifer at grass, and bellow as bulls;"* Jer. 50:11.

Some prophesies to come:

"I will utterly consume all things from off the land, saith the LORD. I will consume man and beast; I will consume the fowls of the heaven, and the fishes of the sea, and the stumblingblocks with the wicked: and I will cut off man from off the land, saith the LORD." Zep. 1:2–3.

"In that day, saith the LORD, I will smite every horse with astonishment, and his rider with madness: and I will open mine eyes upon the house of Judah, and will smite every horse of the people with blindness." Zec. 12:4.

When the days of these prophesies are fulfilled, who would you blame, the person executing the plan or God who planned it and said it shall come to pass? Will some give credit to God while others blame Satan for the same based on how it was fulfilled? You watch: God will raise someone that will execute these plans. He who has all the power and authority over everything deserves both the credit and the blame. Remember, if you give blame to Satan, you've denied God the credit; because God has the power and the will to do in all things. While we wait to the complete understanding of God, as we give credit to Him so also we must give the blame to Him. We cannot say God has authority and power over everything and when it comes to giving credit, we give that to Him. And when it is time to give blame, we look for someone else—Satan.

Questions to Ponder

Who determines the outcome of all events?

Does Satan have power of his own to decide the outcome of any event without being sent by God?

Can anyone succeed without provisions from God?

Chapter Eight

He Tempts

Fundamentals:

*"And it came to pass after these things, that God did tempt Abraham, and said unto him, Abraham: and he said, Behold, here I am. And he said, Take now thy son, thine only son Isaac, whom thou lovest, and get thee into the land of Moriah; and offer him there for a burnt offering upon one of the mountains which I will tell thee of…And Abraham stretched forth his hand, and took the knife to slay his son. And the angel of the LORD called unto him out of heaven, and said, Abraham, Abraham: and he said, Here am I. And he said, Lay not thine hand upon the lad, neither do thou any thing unto him: **for now I know** that thou fearest God, seeing thou hast not withheld thy son, thine only son from me." Gen. 22:1–2 and 22:10–12.*

"I also will not henceforth drive out any from before them of the nations which Joshua left when he died: That through them I may prove Israel, whether they will keep the way of the LORD to walk therein, as their fathers did keep it, or not. Therefore the LORD left those nations, without driving them out hastily; neither delivered he them into the hand of Joshua." Jdg. 2:21–23.

Several have undertaken with courage to explore and/or exploit some of the revelations given to mankind by God, most especially in the matter of whether or not God tempts or tests man. Therefore, since

I myself have carefully studied the Bible, I find it necessary to give you an illustration in this matter. This chapter covers the subject of temptation and test—who is making the temptation and who wants to know the outcome of the temptations and tests. Why would God tempt or test you?

Who Wants to Know?

Many have been convinced that God knows everything, including the thoughts of man. If that is the case, why then will God tempt man to know what man will do or what man thinks? Some have concluded also that God tempts man for man to know where he stands. By principle, it is the tester that wants to know if the testee meets a certain criteria the tester has set as a base for a pass. In the days of Abraham, God tempted Abraham to know if Abraham had any reservation towards Him as He dealt with him—the temptation was for Abraham to sacrifice his only legal son Isaac. *"And he said, Lay not thine hand upon the lad, neither do thou any thing unto him: **for now I know** that thou fearest God, seeing thou hast not withheld thy son, thine only son from me."*

Abraham passed the temptation or test by not having any reservation as he dealt with God in preparation and readiness to use his only son Isaac for a burnt offering as God had instructed him. What was God trying to demonstrate? Obviously He was not trying to make Abraham know what Abraham already knew. God Himself wanted to know if Abraham was willing to give up everything and anything to show total submission to God. Abraham demonstrated a complete surrender and was rewarded with complete trust from God—he was credited with righteousness. Many have stated in the past and even today that God does not tempt man, despite the scripture stating otherwise. The scripture also said God does not tempt man because He knows what is in a man. God may know quite well what is in a man; why then will He tempt or test man?

This manner of God testing what He has created or made can also be seen in the life of Jeremiah the prophet. When the word of the Lord came to Jeremiah that he had been set apart to become a prophet, Jeremiah cried out saying: *"...I do not know how to speak; I am only a child."* Jeremiah 1:6 NIV. Then God touched his mouth so that he could speak the wisdom of God. And God tested or validated Jeremiah: "The word of the Lord came to me: "What do you see, Jeremiah?" "I see

The Acts of God

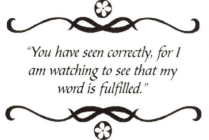

"You have seen correctly, for I am watching to see that my word is fulfilled."

the branch of an almond tree," I replied. The Lord said to me, **"You have seen correctly, for I am watching to see that my word is fulfilled."** Jeremiah 1:11–12 NIV. It was after then that God began to show Jeremiah what He (God) was about to do. God periodically if not frequently does test His creations.

Job was considered blameless, perfect, and upright in his ways, it was God who sent or allowed Satan to go and test Job. What was the purpose of God sending Satan to test Job? It was to show whether Job would remain steadfast either in wealth, in riches, or in lack.

In the matter of the Promised Land and the Israelites, God said to the Israelites that He was keeping some of the inhabitants of the land to test if the next generations to come would keep His ways. *"I also will not henceforth drive out any from before them of the nations which Joshua left when he died: That through them **I may prove Israel, whether they will keep the way of the LORD to walk therein, as their fathers did keep it, or not**. Therefore the LORD left those nations, without driving them out hastily; neither delivered he them into the hand of Joshua."* Jdg. 2:21–23. The question then is this, in the matter referenced, who wanted to know? Was it God who wanted to know, or the Israelites? I'll tell you the truth, it was God. Note also that God wanted to use these people to strengthen the next generations of the Israelites in warfare.

God will tempt you! I mean God will test you. I mean God will strengthen you. I mean God wants to know. I mean God does do validation on His creations. In the beginning when God made the initial creations (light, sea, water, and so on), the Bible says that "God saw that it was good." That means that He validated it somehow before making such statement—"God saw." I say it again: God will tempt you!

For your comfort, the testing and temptations from God come to strengthen us in all areas of life. Sometimes, the one being tested or tempted may not be the beneficiary or the one that is being strengthened, but rather someone else.

Questions to Ponder

What was the purpose of Satan testing Job?

Will God tempt or test you?

What is the purpose of your trials and temptations?

Chapter Nine

He is Merciful

Fundamentals:

"...to give thee great and goodly cities, which thou buildedst not, And houses full of all good things, which thou filledst not, and wells digged, which thou diggedst not, vineyards and olive trees, which thou plantedst not; when thou shalt have eaten and be full;" Deu. 6:10–11.

"And he sent, and brought him in. Now he was ruddy, and withal of a beautiful countenance, and goodly to look to. And the LORD said, Arise, anoint him: for this is he. Then Samuel took the horn of oil, and anointed him in the midst of his brethren: and the Spirit of the LORD came upon David from that day forward..." 1 Sam. 16:12–13.

"...the LORD gave Job twice as much as he had before." Job 42:10.

"Come, and let us return unto the LORD: for he hath torn, and he will heal us; he hath smitten, and he will bind us up." Hos. 6:1.

"For God so loved the world, that he gave his only begotten Son, that whosoever believeth in him should not perish, but have everlasting life." Jn. 3:16.

Despite all that we have shared in the prior chapters, God is still merciful to man. Why? This is because the combination of the good, the bad, and the ugly brings about the complete plan of God. But if our understanding were unwavering, we would see everything as good. Our prior chapters were not to show that God is a bad supernatural being, it was to demonstrate how we humans have misunderstood the ways of God. This chapter will focus on some of the great things God had deposited for us as humans. When combined with the rest of this book, the complete supernatural being of God becomes more apparent.

The Harvest

When Israel was being disciplined, destroyed, and killed during the journey of the exodus, although God dealt with them severely, He led them to harvest where they did not sow, and He did not utterly destroy them from the face of the earth. You may think it was because of the promise He made to their forefathers (Abraham, Isaac, and Jacob). However, this promise was really not a promise if you truly understand the way God manifests His plans. In way of a promise, He revealed to their fathers what He'd do. In fact, what He had stored for them to inherit was beyond promise and treasure: *"...to give thee great and goodly cities, which thou buildedst not, And houses full of all good things, which thou filledst not, and wells digged, which thou diggedst not, vineyards and olive trees, which thou plantedst not; when thou shalt have eaten and be full;"* Deu. 6:10–11. While this was God's blessings to the Israelites, these were, however, properties that belonged to other people. That is, Israel gathered where they did not sow. Israel inherited what did not belong to them. In today's world, this would be called stealing. Did God place the previous inhabitants to build these cities so that the Israelites would come, inherit, and dwell in them? Absolutely! As I pointed out before, Israel faced both difficult times and glorious times while under the promises of God. Their success was partly credited to the fact that they stood firm in the midst of afflictions. For that reason, I would say to you, stand firm with the plan of God in the midst of your afflictions and you'll achieve your victory. Learn how to be positive in everything—this is good for you. Those you call afflictions you would later call them part of your blessings. As some would say, "it was a blessing in disguise." No, it wasn't a blessing in disguise; it was your lack of understanding that caused you not to see the blessing at that time. For this reason, be positive at all times—the level of your harvest would be based on how positive you are at all times. Those positive at all times are more successful than those positive sometimes only. Your harvest is your success.

Only God

How can a sheep keeper become one of the greatest kings the world has ever known? Only God can make such a thing happen, because man would not in his right mind think that a sheep keeper is capable of becoming a king. Many do not realize a sheep keeper is one who is diligent in what he does. Plus, God was looking for a diligent king. So Samuel went and anointed David king of Israel in the house of his father, Jesse. Did God plant David in the shepherd job to prepare and train him before he was anointed king? You bet!

For David to start his internship, Saul had to have invited or employed him into the palace. Note that Saul at this time did not know that David had been anointed king of Israel to takeover the kingship from him. Now Saul needed someone who could play the harp and calm his insanity (for Saul was insane). And it was told to Saul that David, the son of Jesse, knew how to play the harp very well. So Saul sent for David; *"And David came to Saul, and stood before him: and he loved him greatly; and he became his armourbearer."* 1 Sam. 16:21.

"And it came to pass, when the evil spirit from God was upon Saul, that David took an harp, and played with his hand: so Saul was refreshed, and was well, and the evil spirit departed from him." 1 Sam. 16:23. This is how David started his internship at the palace of kings. God is a rewarder of those who do things diligently. A sheep keeper for that matter was made king over a people that were stubborn. God is a merciful God. Though David was anointed when he was a youth, he started to reign when he was thirty years old. Why did it take that long for David to take the throne or kingship after he has been anointed by Samuel to be king over all Israel (Judah and Israel)? *"David was thirty years old when he began to reign, and he reigned forty years. In Hebron he reigned over Judah seven years and six months: and in Jerusalem he reigned thirty and three years over all Israel and Judah."* 2 Sam. 5:4–5. Does it make sense to YOU what David went through before he took

the throne? Wouldn't YOU have said it was a false anointing after all these long years?

Did David undergo training and establish himself during this time in preparation for his kingship? Why then do you think that it took too long? You see, the plans of God are always orderly, whether you understand it or not. Furthermore, it is not only how you start that matters, but also what is in your destiny and whether you complete it.

After Job was chastised by God in every way, almost to the point of death, the Lord restored Job. *"...the LORD gave Job twice as much as he had before."* Job 42:10. Why? Because Job understood how God worked and he never gave up on God. If you stay firm in His ways and plan, good plus bad plus ugly equals the manifestation of God's plan. In all that you're getting, get understanding.

"Come, and let us return unto the LORD: for he hath torn, and he will heal us; he hath smitten, and he will bind us up." Hos. 6:1.

Your Only Sacrifice

"For God so loved the world, that he gave his only begotten Son, that whosoever believeth in him should not perish, but have everlasting life."

The mercy of God for man far outreaches what any man can imagine. God said His people perish for lack of knowledge. So that man may live a life of truth, God sent His only Son to earth to die for us to have an everlasting life—a life only attainable by those who live in truth here on earth. *"For God so loved the world, that he gave his only begotten Son, that whosoever believeth in him should not perish, but have everlasting life."* Jn. 3:16. If you believe in Him (Jesus Christ), then you have acquired the knowledge of truth that will last you forever. For He loves the world so much that He sent His only Son to bring us the truth without contamination. If there's nothing else you can do, at least believe in the truth He has brought for you. There's no other truth out there for which a man can live.

Consider the Lord Jesus and His life; though He came to forgive men their sins and give them everlasting life, He went through a process that cannot be grasped with mere human understanding. Thanks be to God, who reveals His plans to His faithful.

Part of what Jesus demonstrated to us during His lifetime was the complete surrender to what God had created Him to fulfill, whether painful or painless, without having His mind flying around with other selfish desires. The will of God for Him was to come and pay for our sins with His life (very painful). This was the will of God for the most beloved Son Jesus.

Do what you have been created to do, whether painful or painless.

That being said, what value is your life? Very great, because it was purchased with the life of One greater than any one. On the other hand, very little, because if the life of the Lord Jesus was worth sacrificing, yours is nothing—it is only as good as your destiny, whether painful or painless. *"And he went forward a little, and fell on the ground, and prayed that, if it were possible, the hour might pass from him. And he said, Abba, Father, all things are possible unto thee; take away this cup from me: nevertheless not what I will, but what thou wilt."* Mk. 14:35–36. What would have happened if the Lord Jesus had walked away or attempted to walk away from His divine purpose? Think about it.

So whether the will of God for your life is to serve painfully or painlessly, do it faithfully. The will of God for Jesus' coming was to die on the cross in order that we may know the truth in this manner about the Kingdom of God. That is, painful or painless, just do it. Your life is only worth what it is made for. Jesus knew that was the only important thing in life, and He stood to face death rather than walking away from the will of the Father who sent Him. *Do what you have been created to do, whether painful or painless*—let your goal be to fulfill what God has created you for. If you do, even in pain, you'll claim victory.

Questions to Ponder

How grateful are you for who you are?

How are you partaking of the grace and mercy of God?

Have you found your God-given purpose?

Conclusion

Every human on the planet earth is likened unto a man-made spacecraft sent to a distant planet for specific assignments. So also God created and sent man to this planet for specific assignments.

Today, significant progress has been made in the human understanding about the Kingdom of God; mankind's next level of understanding is in the realm of knowledge—"The Knowledge Age." However, the ultimate goal is yet to be reached. Mankind's ultimate goal for understanding is "The Wisdom Age"—the level of understanding that is equivalent to how God works and does things. Those who attain this level of understanding during their lifetime are worry- and stress-free; because they have the wisdom of God and lack no understanding. These people are wise to the point that they have no downside and upside; they're always in a rejoicing state. Their perception of things are always good. Whether they have little or much, they are in good spirit. Whether in riches, in wealth, or in lack, they are in good spirit. Whether they had been beaten, afflicted, or hard pressed, they are in good spirit. Knowing that every step of life is planned by God to fulfill His BIG plan would stir up your spirit. Rather than seeing some things as good, bad, or ugly, you will instead see: God the good, the grace, and the blessings—and your joy will be full.

When Job was afflicted almost to the point of death, Job said, who doesn't know the hand of the Lord is doing these things? And because he understood how the Kingdom works, he stayed firm and was rewarded in the end. *"...the LORD gave Job twice as much as he had before."* Job 42:10. He alleged all creations know the Lord did these:

"But ask now the beasts, and they shall teach thee; and the fowls of the air, and they shall tell thee: Or speak to the earth, and it shall teach thee: and the fishes of the sea shall declare unto thee. Who knoweth not in all these that the hand of the LORD hath wrought this? In whose hand is the soul of every living thing, and the breath of all mankind. Doth not the ear try words? and the mouth taste his meat? With the ancient is wisdom; and in length of days understanding. With him is wisdom and strength, he hath counsel and understanding. Behold, he breaketh down, and it cannot be built again: he shutteth up a man, and there can be no opening. Behold, he withholdeth the waters, and they dry up: also he sendeth them out, and they overturn the earth. With him is strength and wisdom: the deceived and the deceiver are his. He leadeth counsellors away spoiled, and maketh the judges fools. He looseth the bond of kings, and girdeth their loins with a girdle. He leadeth princes away spoiled, and overthroweth the mighty. He removeth away the speech of the trusty, and taketh away the understanding of the aged. He poureth contempt upon princes, and weakeneth the strength of the mighty. He discovereth deep things out of darkness, and bringeth out to light the shadow of death. He increaseth the nations, and destroyeth them: he enlargeth the nations, and straiteneth them again. He taketh away the heart of the chief of the people of the earth, and causeth them to wander in a wilderness where there is no way. They grope in the dark without light, and he maketh them to stagger like a drunken man." Job 12:7–25.

Despite all his afflictions, Job said, *"Though he slay me, yet will I trust in him: but I will maintain mine own ways before him."* Job 13:15.

I hope all these events and activities referenced throughout the book had been able to improve your understanding that every step of life's progress was predestined by God. We were able to establish that God according to His good will, created every thing not just some things. Furthermore, we concluded that God is the cause of all events and not just some events—whether the impression you and I have on that creation is good, bad or ugly. We further used the magnificent story of Joseph to demonstrate how the steps in the plans of God may at times seem bad in our eyes and after it is finished, it was not bad as we thought it was. We also talked about the aspect of God's cursings and how we as humans need to change the way we think about those commands of God that we perceived as curse. Furthermore, we discussed the fact that God would wound or afflict you regardless of whether you are His favorite or not—afflictions will come and they are part of life process if you have the understanding—Jesus had this understanding and He rejoiced all the way to death. We also established the fact that despite all His creations, God is also the creator of death which takes away the creations. And death indeed comes in various forms ordained by God. Being that many in our human race had come and gone without the understanding that various things we blame others for are as a result of ignorance, it was necessary to discuss the credit and blame game—and discuss we did! Blaming others had limited our ability to give God the credit. We therefore established that if it is difficult for us to recognize and give God the credit, we must not give the blame to someone else other than God. We also touched on that least discussed topic, whether God tempts or test His creations. Lastly, we looked into the mercy of God and what is in it for us in the midst of all these chaos.

Perhaps, someone may ask, how did we get ourselves into such a messy confusion and misunderstanding of God and His ways? I would say to that person, you are not alone. Many had unintentionally disregarded the word of God. Others had deliberately disregarded the word and had gotten smarter in their own eyes without the knowledge of God and had been able to deceive others with it. As a result, they are both set for eternal condemnation. As I mentioned earlier, God created us in His likeness. This means that, we have a spirit in us that is self-centered—thinking about self first. The same way the plans of God are centered around Him. You have to understand that the plans of God are centered around Him and not around you. Our challenge is to overcome that self-centeredness and do what God wants us to do because He had created us to work for Him or to be His co-laborers. It is not that our choice in that self-centered thinking would manifest over the plans of God, but rather it is a way for us to stimulate our minds. However as God said about the Babylonians, though they did what He commissioned them to do, their hearts were not right when they did it. Do what you're commissioned to do and be thankful always without letting your mind drift away from the commission because of personal desire.

The combination of all these good, bad, and ugly events and activities, your task and mine, from creation to death brings about the complete plan of God.

"So then, those who suffer according to God's will should commit themselves to their faithful creator and continue to do good" 1 Pet. 4:19 NIV.

"Rejoice in the Lord alway: and again I say, Rejoice. Let your moderation be known unto all men. The Lord is at hand. Be careful for nothing; but in every thing by prayer and supplication with thanksgiving let your requests be made known unto God. And the peace of God, which passeth all understanding, shall keep your hearts and minds through Christ Jesus." Php. 4:4–7.

"Both the deceived and the deceiver are His."

Rejoice always, at all times, in everything. Why? Because God is the author of everything. You may not understand your situations; however, it is the Lord's doing, and therefore you should rejoice. The Lord knows what He's doing! He has not created one bad thing—because after finished creating, He confirmed that they were good. *"Both the deceived and the deceiver are His."* You must have a positive attitude about everything!

God has created everything and has placed each person according to His purpose and to fulfill His plans (not yours). If you lack these underlying principles, you will find yourself seeing, hearing, and sensing some things as good, others as bad and/or ugly. Note however that this is your perception, not how God made them—He made everything good.

Fulfilling God's Plan for Your Life

In Revelation 4:11, the Bible says that God created all things, and for His pleasure we were created and have our being. You may ask, what life must I live to please God? What life must I live to fulfill my God-given destiny? What life must I live to fulfill God's plan for my life? To accomplish all these, you must first acknowledge Jesus Christ as your Lord

The Acts of God

"This is the work of God, that ye believe on him whom he hath sent."

and Savior—*"This is the work of God, that ye believe on him whom he hath sent."* Jn. 6:29. You must acknowledge that God exists. The Bible says that those who come to God must acknowledge that He exists and He rewards those who diligently seek Him. *"But without faith it is impossible to please him: for he that cometh to God must believe that he is, and that he is a rewarder of them that diligently seek him."* Heb. 11:6. What does this mean—without faith? *"Now faith is the substance of things hoped for, the evidence of things not seen."* Heb. 11:1. That you believed even though you do not physically see what you hope or had been promised. As my pastor appropriately puts it: "Faith is the only currency or legal tender in which heaven transacts." Without faith, you cannot please God or receive from Him—you must believe what Jesus had said about God and His kingdom. Many people agree and use the teaching Jesus gave; however, they have not profess publicly that He is Lord of their lives. Jesus said, if you deny Him among men, He would deny you in the presence of God. I say to those people, the grace was given free of charge—take it! Because in the second coming of Jesus Christ—when the dead and the living saints would be lifted up to heaven, the prize would be given not by grace but according to what each man has done. *"And, behold, I come quickly; and my reward is with me, to give every man according as his work shall be. I am Alpha and Omega, the beginning and the end, the first and the last."* Rev. 22:12-13. This leads us to our next point.

There are qualities we must possess and uphold in addition to the faith we profess in order to attain that prize we hope for. They had been summarized in this manner by Peter: *"According as his divine power hath given unto us all things that pertain unto life and godliness, through the knowledge of him that hath called us to glory and virtue: Whereby are given unto us exceeding great and precious promises: that by these ye might be partakers of the divine nature, having escaped the corruption that is in the world through lust.* ***And beside this, giving all diligence, add to your faith virtue; and to virtue knowledge; And to knowledge***

temperance; and to temperance patience; and to patience godliness; And to godliness brotherly kindness; and to brotherly kindness charity. *For if these things be in you, and abound, they make you that ye shall neither be barren nor unfruitful in the knowledge of our Lord Jesus Christ. But he that lacketh these things is blind, and cannot see afar off, and hath forgotten that he was purged from his old sins. Wherefore the rather, brethren, give diligence to make your calling and election sure: for if ye do these things, ye shall never fall: For so an entrance shall be ministered unto you abundantly into the everlasting kingdom of our Lord and Saviour Jesus Christ."* 2 Pet. 1:3-11. Your faith in Jesus Christ and these qualities would determine whether you would be selected to spend your life in heaven or in hell. As Jesus affirmed, your destination would be based on what you have done here on earth.

Looking for a life to emulate? Emulate that of Christ, because He demonstrated a life filled with joy, peace, love, completeness, fulfillment, obedience, longsuffering, and total submission to the will of the Father (God) who sent Him. Who sent YOU?

Therefore,
"Love the Lord thy God with all thy heart."
"Love thy neighbor as thyself"

Get started: pick up a Bible, start reading with the gospel of John and find yourself a Bible-based church. If you have already started, stand firm—because those who fall away would not inherit the kingdom of God. He is coming soon.

God bless!!!

Made in the USA
Lexington, KY
24 May 2014